P9-AFT-263

Know your furniture parts.

Here's how it all comes together.

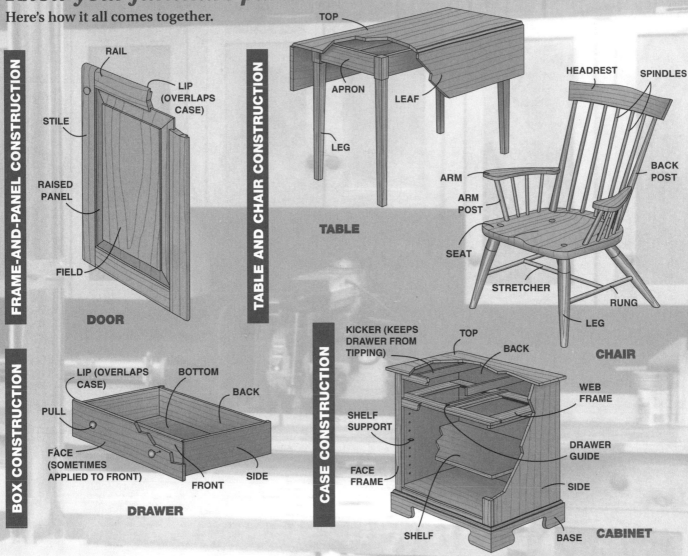

FRAME-AND-PANEL CONSTRUCTION

RAIL
LIP (OVERLAPS CASE)
STILE
RAISED PANEL
FIELD

DOOR

BOX CONSTRUCTION

LIP (OVERLAPS CASE)
BOTTOM
BACK
PULL
FACE (SOMETIMES APPLIED TO FRONT)
FRONT
SIDE

DRAWER

TABLE AND CHAIR CONSTRUCTION

TOP
APRON
LEAF
LEG

TABLE

HEADREST
SPINDLES
ARM
ARM POST
BACK POST
SEAT
STRETCHER
RUNG
LEG

CHAIR

CASE CONSTRUCTION

KICKER (KEEPS DRAWER FROM TIPPING)
TOP
BACK
WEB FRAME
SHELF SUPPORT
DRAWER GUIDE
FACE FRAME
SIDE
SHELF
BASE

CABINET

Know your decorative shapes.

These are the elements of woodworking style.

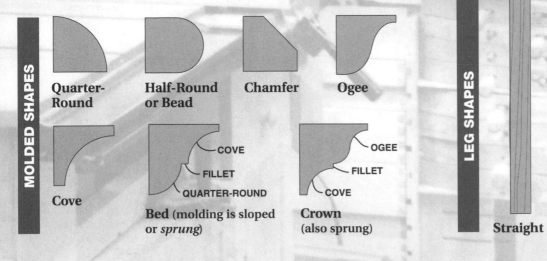

MOLDED SHAPES

Quarter-Round

Half-Round or Bead

Chamfer

Ogee

Cove

Bed (molding is sloped or *sprung*)
— COVE
— FILLET
— QUARTER-ROUND

Crown (also sprung)
OGEE
FILLET
COVE

LEG SHAPES

POST
KNEE
ANKLE
FOOT

Straight   Tapered   Cabriole

SECRETS OF SUCCESSFUL WOODWORKING™

TEACHING YOUR ROUTER NEW TRICKS

SECRETS OF SUCCESSFUL WOODWORKING™

TEACHING YOUR ROUTER NEW TRICKS

Nick Engler

Rodale Press, Inc.
Emmaus, Pennsylvania

OUR PURPOSE

*"We inspire and enable people to improve
their lives and the world around them."*

©1998 by Bookworks, Inc.
Published by Rodale Press, Inc.
By arrangement with Bookworks, Inc.

All rights reserved. No part of this publication may be
reproduced or transmitted in any form or by any means,
electronic or mechanical, including photocopy, recording,
or any other information storage and retrieval system,
without the written permission of the publisher, with the
following exception:

Rodale Press grants permission to photocopy patterns
to persons making the projects for their own personal use.

The author and editors who compiled this book have tried
to make all of the contents as accurate and as correct as
possible. Plans, illustrations, photographs, and text have
all been carefully checked and cross-checked. However,
due to the variability of local conditions, construction
materials, personal skill, and so on, neither the author nor
Rodale Press assumes any responsibility for any injuries
suffered or for damages or other losses incurred that result
from the material presented herein. All instructions and
plans should be carefully studied and clearly understood
before beginning construction.

Printed in the United States of America on acid-free ∞,
recycled ♻ paper

**The Library of Congress has cataloged Volume 1
as follows:**

Engler, Nick.
        Making flawless cabinets and built-ins / Nick Engler.
        p.   cm.   (Secrets of successful
    woodworking ; #1)
        Includes bibliographical references and index.
        ISBN 0–87596–805–8   (Vol. 1 hardcover)
        1. Woodwork.   2. Cabinetwork.   3. Built-in
    furniture.   I. Title.   II. Series: Engler, Nick. Secrets of
    successful woodworking ; #1.
        TT180.E645   1998
        684.1'6—ddc21   98–8912

Vol. 2 ISBN 0–87596–817–1

Distributed in the book trade by St. Martin's Press

2 4 6 8 10 9 7 5 3 1   hardcover

Bookworks Staff
Designer: Linda Watts
Illustrator and Project Designer: Mary Jane Favorite
Art assistance: David Van Etten
Interior and Back Cover Photographer: Karen Callahan
Master Craftsman: Jim McCann
Indexer: Beverly Bremer
Chief Executive Officer: Robert C. Sammons

Rodale Press Home and Garden Books Staff
Vice President and Editorial Director: Margaret J. Lydic
Managing Editor, Woodworking Books: Rick Peters
Editor: Tony O'Malley
Director of Design and Production: Michael Ward
Associate Art Director: Carol Angstadt
Cover Designer and design assistance: Dale Mack
Front Cover Photographer: Mitch Mandel
Photo Editor: James A. Gallucci
Studio Manager: Leslie M. Keefe
Copy Director: Dolores Plikaitis
Copy Editor: Barbara McIntosh Webb
Manufacturing Manager: Mark Krahforst
Manufacturing Coordinator: Patrick T. Smith
Office Manager: Karen Earl-Braymer

Special Thanks to:

Larry Callahan
West Milton, Ohio

Judy Ditmer
Piqua, Ohio

Scott Harrold
Miamisburg, Ohio

Wertz Stores
West Milton, Ohio

Workshops of David T. Smith
Morrow, Ohio

Barbara and Glen Wuest
Milwaukee, Wisconsin

We're always happy to hear from you. For questions or
comments concerning the editorial content of this book,
please write to:

Rodale Press, Inc.
Book Readers' Service
33 East Minor Street
Emmaus, PA 18098

Look for other Rodale books wherever books are sold.
Or call us at (800) 848-4735.

For more information about Rodale Press and the books
and magazines we publish, visit our World Wide Web
site at:

http://www.rodalepress.com

The Incredible Router

The router is like a Swiss army knife for your woodworking shop. There is no other power tool that is as versatile and capable. It serves as both a portable and a stationary power tool and can be used for anything from making wood joints to cutting intricate shapes and profiles. With a few simple jigs and fixtures, the router becomes a plane, a circle cutter, a mortising machine, and a dozen other tools.

I've written this book to help you explore the versatility and capability of your router. This is not just a book of routing *techniques,* although it explains all major routing operations. And it's not just a routing *projects* book, although there are complete plans and instructions for five handsome routing projects plus a router table. It's not an *idea* book, although you'll find photographs of many different projects built by craftsmen from all over America with their routers. It's not a book of router *jigs and fixtures,* although you'll find plenty of them. It's *all of these* — and something completely different.

This is a step-by-step description of what it took for a band of craftsmen to design and build the five routing projects shown here. It shows not just how to use the router, but *how to integrate it with the other tools in your shop.*

Teaching Your Router New Tricks starts out with a small chest, the **Mule Chest.** This shows you how to use the router to make a variety of wood joints, including rabbets, dadoes, grooves, lock joints, and dovetail joints. With the **Writing Table,** we explain how to rout the strongest of all woodworking joints, the mortise-and-tenon. We also use the router to create a simple profile — the thumbnail edge around the tabletop. The **Grandfather Clock** is an exercise in shaping. We use the router to create all manner of molding, both simple and complex, straight and curved.

The **Loaves and Fishes Display Shelves** shows how to create a routing template and duplicate intricate patterns and designs. Finally, the **Victorian Oak Mantel** explains two more uses for the router. We show how to use the router in an *architectural* project for your home, routing the molded profiles needed to create the mantel. We also demonstrate how to use the router to cut beads and flutes in a lathe turning.

Now and then, I leave the story (briefly) to show you a *Quick Fixture* that will extend the capabilities of your router or improve its accuracy. Or to impart some useful *Shop Savvy* or *Methods of Work.* For example:

- A **trammel jig** lets you use your router to cut perfect circles and ovals.
- A **dado-and-rabbet guide** helps position and guide the router when cutting multiple joints.
- An **indexing jig** holds a lathe turning while you rout it, and it enables you to rotate the turning a precise number of degrees between each pass with the router.
- A **planing jig** makes it possible to surface figured wood and flatten warped boards with your router.

The most important routing accessory is, by far, a **router table;** here again, I've done something different. Instead of giving you just a plan, I've broken the router table down into its important components — work table, fence, stand, storage compartment, and so on. Jim McCann, a respected tool designer and engineer, and I explore each component and explain options for making each one. This allows you to *customize* a router table for your woodworking needs.

I've written the book this way because the router isn't the only tool in our shops. We use it in combination with other tools to create woodworking projects. Additionally, no two woodworkers use a router in exactly the same way. I've shown you a wide range of possibilities so you can take advantage of those that strike your fancy.

With all good wishes,

Nick

Contents

MULE CHEST   2

What size should it be?   3

Designing for Easy Access   4

Standard Sizes for Chests and Boxes   4

What style will it be?   5

Other Variations   7

Materials List   8

How do I build it?   9

Preparing the Materials   9

Planing Figured Wood   9

Shop Savvy:
Wrapping a Board around a Box   9

Quick Fixture:
Router Planing Jig   10

Making the Box Joinery   12

Methods of Work:
Routing Rabbets, Dadoes, and Grooves   14

Quick Fixture:
Dado-and-Rabbet Jig   17

Routing Through Dovetails   18

Methods of Work:
Routing Through Dovetails   18

Quick Fixture:
Through Dovetail Template   19

Quick Fixture:
Dovetail Dust Collector   22

No Problem:
Fixing Sloppy Dovetails   23

Assembling the Box   24

Making a Breadboard Lid   25

Hinging the Lid on the Box   26

Quick Fixture:
Hinge-Mortising Jig   26

Making the Drawer   27

Methods of Work:
Making Lock Joints   28

Quick Fixture:
Scratch Bead   28

Shop Savvy:
Pro Router Secrets   29

WRITING TABLE   30

What size should it be?   31

Standard Sizes for Occasional and
Specialty Tables   32

Shop Savvy:
Table Ergonomics   32

What style will it be?   33

Materials List   34

How do I build it?   35

Preparing the Materials   35

No Problem:
Jointing with a Router   35

Joining Legs and Aprons   37

Methods of Work:
Routing Mortises and Tenons   38

Quick Fixture:
Mortising Template   39

Quick Fixture:
Router Table Tenoning Jig   40

Turning the Table Legs   41

Methods of Work:
Duplicating Turned Legs   42

Quick Fixture:
Fixed Calipers   42

Making the Table Top   43

Making and Fitting the Drawer   44

Assembling the Table   45

Finishing the Table   45

Another Way to Go:
Routing Round and Oval Table Tops   46

Quick Fixture:
Router Trammel Jig   49

GRANDFATHER CLOCK   50

What size should it be?   51

What style will it be?   53

Materials List   54

How do I build it?   57

Getting Started   59

Planning Your Attack   61

Making the Base   61

Methods of Work:
Making Bracket Feet   63

Making the Waist   66

Methods of Work:
Routing Molded Shapes   67

Quick Fixtures:
Long Pusher   68
Featherboard   68

Methods of Work:
Routing Spline Grooves   69

Making the Hood   70

Finishing the Clock   73

LOAVES AND FISHES DISPLAY SHELVES   74

What size should it be?   75

Standard Shelving Dimensions   76

What style will it be?   77

Materials List   78

How do I build it?   79

Preparing the Materials   79

Cutting the Joinery   80

Routing Decorative Patterns   81

Making the Valance, Braces, and Moldings   82

Shop Savvy:
Pattern-Routing Techniques   83

Another Way to Go:
Pin Routing   84

Quick Fixture:
Pin-Routing Attachment   85

Assembling the Shelves   86

Shop Savvy:
Saber Saw Sanding   87

VICTORIAN OAK MANTEL   88

What size should it be?   89

Cabinet or Cutout?   90

What style will it be?   91

Materials List   92

How do I build it?   93

Preparing the Materials   93

Shop Savvy:
Routing Hardwoods and Sheet Materials   93

Making the Boxes   95

Methods of Work:
Routing Raised Panels   96

Turning the Column   97

Quick Fixture:
Fluting Jig   99

Shop Savvy:
Routing Turnings and Cylinders   100

Shaping the Moldings and Edges   102

Installing the Boxes   103

Shop Savvy:
Cutting Cove Molding   104

Quick Fixture:
Parallel Rule   104

Applying the Decorative Elements   105

Finishing the Mantel   106

No Problem:
Repairing a Miter Joint   106

Alternatives:
Making a Bump-Out   107

PERSONALIZED ROUTER TABLE   108

Torsion-Box Work Surface   110

Depth-of-Cut Adjusters   113

Quick Fixtures:
Router Crank   113
Router Jack   113

Router Table Fence   114

Fence Stops   116

Starter Pin and Guard   116

Guard and Depth Gauge   117

Fence-Positioning Scales   117

Tilt-Top Stand   118

Storage Cabinet   120

INDEX   122

Mule Chest

In this chapter...

PRACTICAL KNOW-HOW

Making the Box Joinery	12
Routing Rabbets, Dadoes, and Grooves	14
Routing Through Dovetails	18
Routing Hinge Mortises	26
Making Lock Joints	28

JIGS AND FIXTURES

Dado-and-Rabbet Jig	17
Through Dovetail Template	19
Scratch Bead	28

SHOP SOLUTIONS

Planing Figured Wood	9
Wrapping a Board around a Box	9
Fixing Sloppy Dovetails	23
Router Secrets	29

You're probably wondering why this is called a "mule chest." Well, it has nothing to do with pack animals. The name caught on shortly after furniture makers began to manufacture chests with a single drawer in the late sixteenth century. At that time, *mules* were a common type of bedroom slipper. These old-time one-drawer chests were quite large and were commonly used to stored bedding. The drawer (then called a *drawing box*) beneath the bedding compartment (or *till*) was a handy place to store your mules. Fascinating, huh?

Small chests such as these were also referred to as "keeping boxes" — that name, I think, requires no explanation. They are still useful today for keeping a variety of small objects — jewelry, baseball cards, photos, compact discs, and so on. Jim and I made this as a present for a good friend, a man who appreciates tobacco, and we lined it with Spanish cedar so he could use it as a humidor.

It was a routing project from beginning to end, as small chests commonly are. We used the router not only to shape and cut joinery but also to plane the figured wood and to cut recesses for hardware.

What size should it be?

Before we get into routing techniques, however, there's the small matter of designing the chest to fit your needs. The first question you must settle on the road to a usable design is what size to make the chest.

That, of course, depends a good deal on what you want to store in it. If you plan to put jewelry in it, the chest needn't be any larger than the one we built. If you want it to store blankets and bedding, it should be much larger.

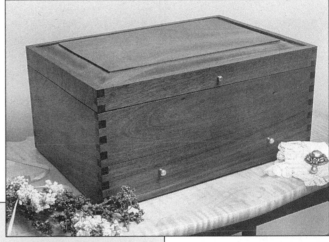

The small chest shown above was sized to hold a modest collection of jewelry — 16 inches long, 10 inches wide, and 10 inches deep. The blanket chest to the left must be larger to hold bedding — 39 × 24 × 24 inches. But the profiles of both chests are *golden rectangles.* This is a rectangle in which the ratio of the height to the length is 1 to 1.618. Ancient Greek architects found that this ratio created especially pleasing proportions, and it's been used to design buildings and furniture ever since.

Crafted by Tom Stender, Boston, NY

DESIGNING FOR EASY ACCESS

No matter what the size of the chest, you must design it for easy access. Whatever you store in it should be easy to find and easy to retrieve. Make the chest too wide or too deep, and it will be difficult to reach items near the bottom of the till. If you're making a small chest, or a chest with small compartments, there should be adequate room to get your fingers around whatever you want to pick up.

If the chest is large or holds many items, you may find yourself rooting through the objects in the chest to find whatever's on the bottom. You may want to devise a better method for finding and retrieving stuff from the interior. When Jim and I lined the chest, we made stacking trays that fit the till. To get at the cigars at the bottom of the till, you simply lift out the trays above them.

Or you can make a *sliding* tray. The tray is only half as large as the interior length or width of the chest and rests on rails. To reach whatever is below the chest, you just slide the tray to one side. This arrangement is used frequently in blanket chests and tool boxes.

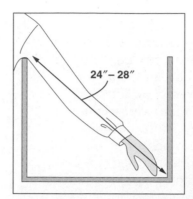

The reach of an adult is generally about 24 to 28 inches from the shoulder. This should be the maximum *diagonal* dimension of the till, as measured from front to back.

A tray in the top of the till in this keeping box holds small items. To get at objects below, simply lift the tray out.

STANDARD SIZES FOR CHESTS AND BOXES

A box or a chest can be built to any practical size, as long as it's easy to reach the items in the interior or till. However, specific types of chests usually fall within a given range.

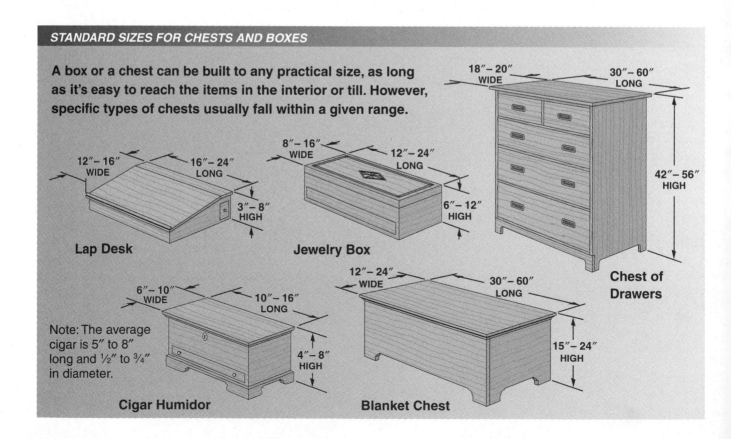

Lap Desk — 12"–16" WIDE, 16"–24" LONG, 3"–8" HIGH

Jewelry Box — 8"–16" WIDE, 12"–24" LONG, 6"–12" HIGH

Chest of Drawers — 18"–20" WIDE, 30"–60" LONG, 42"–56" HIGH

Note: The average cigar is 5" to 8" long and ½" to ¾" in diameter.

Cigar Humidor — 6"–10" WIDE, 10"–16" LONG, 4"–8" HIGH

Blanket Chest — 12"–24" WIDE, 30"–60" LONG, 15"–24" HIGH

What style will it be?

In addition to being a useful and attractive storage piece, the mule chest has an interesting history. It was an important step in the evolution of the furniture we commonly use today, both at work and at home.

A BRIEF HISTORY OF CHESTS The mule chest itself descended from what is perhaps the oldest storage device — the box. Medieval boxes and chests were typically made from six thick boards joined together — what we remember today as a six-board chest. These offered a lot of storage space, but they weren't particularly user-friendly. The owners soon found that it was tedious to dig through the stuff at the top of the till to reach the stuff on the bottom. But they put up with this shortcoming for a few centuries until some enterprising Renaissance furniture maker decided to put a box inside the box. He mounted a lidless box in the bottom of the till so it could be drawn out of the front of the chest. *Ta-da!* A "drawing box." (Later shortened to *drawer.*)

Well, if one drawing box was a good idea, then two should be even better, right? They were.

Adding a third and fourth drawing box worked pretty well, too. Before another century had passed, furniture makers were filling an entire chest with drawing boxes. This new furniture form was called the *chest of drawers.*

It went little noticed at the time, but this was a development that ranked right up there with sliced bread and the assembly line. Try to imagine your life without drawers — not just your bedroom and your kitchen, but your workplace as well. From the chest of drawers, we derived the desk and the filing cabinet, the playing fields on which all the business in the world is conducted.

While this was happening, the six-board chest and mule chest found new uses and continued to be popular storage pieces. Consequently, you can find examples of chests in almost any style. The chest shown on page 2 is done in a classic Queen Anne style, popular in the mid-eighteenth century. However, simply by changing the design of the feet and the molded edges, you can make many different styles. Here are a few examples.

Courtesy Harry L. Smith, Kunkletown, PA ; photo by John Bender

PENNSYLVANIA GERMAN STYLE

Study the profile of this piece, and you'll find it's very similar to the mule chest in this chapter. That's because it was made during the Queen Anne era, and the craftsman who built it was probably influenced by the prevailing designs of the time. However, unlike the mule chest, the surfaces are intricately painted. This is the mark of the Pennsylvania German style. Immigrant German and Swiss craftsmen banded together in conservative communities outside Philadelphia to preserve their Old World traditions, among them a style of furniture adorned by brightly painted folk designs.

SCROLLWORK STYLE

Not all boxes have to completely enclose the space they define, as this intricate scrollwork box by Peter Holt shows. The open spaces in the top and sides of the box create a lace-like pattern. Scrollwork (or *fretwork,* as it is sometimes called) is descended from a decorative Victorian woodworking technique known as Sorrento wood carving, after a town in Italy where craftsmen developed it into a high art.

Crafted by Peter Holt, Chattanooga, TN

STUDIO STYLE

The Studio or *Handicraft Revival* style is the collective name for the riot of highly individual designs that are being built today. If there is any central theme at all, it's technique. Studio craftsmen have invented many new woodworking techniques and have pushed traditional methods to new frontiers. Jim built this keeping box just to push routing technique as far as he could. In addition to the joinery, all the decorative splines and inlays were made with a router.

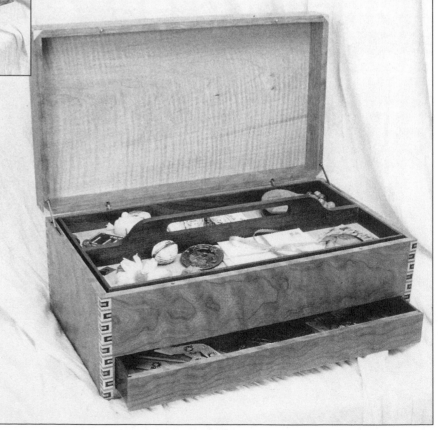

OTHER VARIATIONS

In addition to varying the size and style, you might also vary the configuration in which the components are put together. By doing so, you can create other useful storage pieces.

MACHINIST'S TOOL CHEST

This beauty is Jim's personal tool chest, which he made from a single piece of curly birch. (Jim once worked for H. Gerstner & Sons, who manufacture some of the finest wooden tool chests in the world.) This, too, is a variation on the mule chest. But instead of a single large drawer, there are many small ones. The depth of the till has been reduced to create room for the additional drawers and to make it easier to retrieve the tools stored in it.

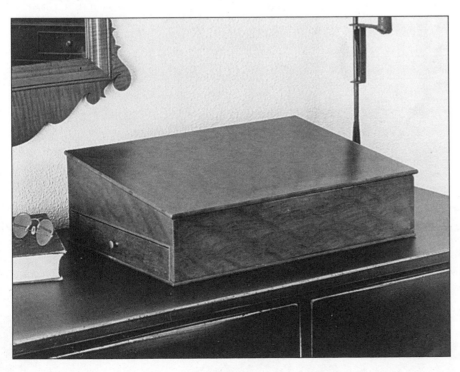

LAP DESK

This elegant lap desk, an exact reproduction of a historic Shaker piece, was made by David T. Smith and was featured in the book *American Country Furniture*, which David and my wife and I wrote several years ago. This piece has exactly the same components as the mule chest: It's a box with a lid and a single drawer. But the lid is slanted to serve as a writing surface, and the drawer pulls out from the side so you can reach the materials inside when the piece is resting on your lap.

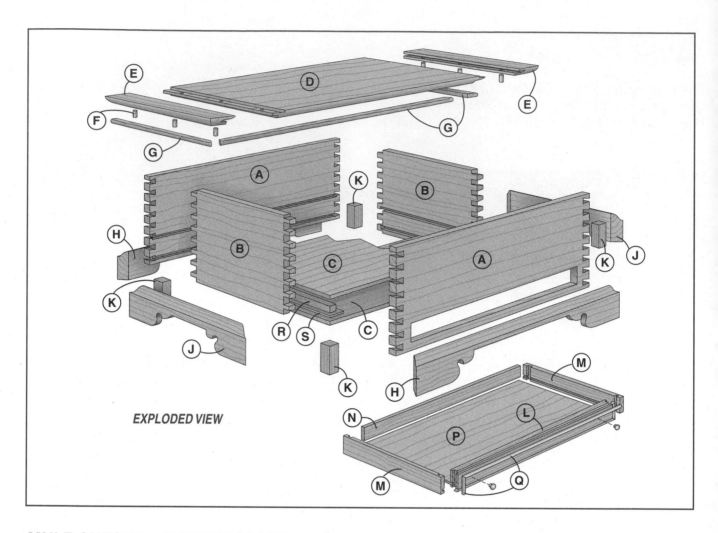

EXPLODED VIEW

MULE CHEST ■ *MATERIALS LIST* (Finished Dimensions)

PARTS

A	Front/back (2)	$\frac{1}{2}" \times 8" \times 16"$
B	Sides (2)	$\frac{1}{2}" \times 8" \times 8"$
C	Bottoms (2)	$\frac{1}{4}" \times 15\frac{1}{2}" \times 7\frac{3}{8}"$
D	Lid	$\frac{5}{8}" \times 8\frac{7}{8}" \times 16\frac{1}{4}"$
E	Breadboards (2)	$\frac{5}{8}" \times 1\frac{1}{4}" \times 8\frac{7}{8}"$
F	Dowels (6)	$\frac{3}{16}"$ dia. $\times \frac{1}{2}"$
G	Lid molding (total)	$\frac{1}{4}" \times \frac{3}{8}" \times 36"$
H	Base front/back (2)	$\frac{1}{2}" \times 2\frac{1}{2}" \times 17"$
J	Base sides (2)	$\frac{1}{2}" \times 2\frac{1}{2}" \times 9"$
K	Glue blocks (4)	$\frac{1}{2}" \times \frac{1}{2}" \times 2"$
L	Drawer front	$\frac{1}{2}" \times 1\frac{1}{2}" \times 14"$
M	Drawer sides (2)	$\frac{1}{4}" \times 1\frac{1}{2}" \times 7\frac{3}{8}"$
N	Drawer back	$\frac{1}{4}" \times 1\frac{1}{4}" \times 13\frac{3}{4}"$
P	Drawer bottom	$\frac{1}{8}" \times 7\frac{1}{8}" \times 13\frac{3}{4}"$
Q	Cock beading (total)	$\frac{1}{8}" \times \frac{1}{4}" \times 32"$

R	Drawer guides (2)	$\frac{1}{2}" \times \frac{1}{2}" \times 7\frac{1}{2}"$
S	Drawer supports (2)	$\frac{1}{8}" \times 1" \times 7\frac{1}{2}"$

HARDWARE

$\frac{1}{2}"$ Drawer pulls (2)

$1" \times 1" \times 1\frac{1}{4}"$ Quadrant hinges (2)

RESOURCES

The pulls and hinges are available from:
    The Woodworkers' Store
    4365 Willow Drive
    Medina, MN 55340
If you want to use this chest as a humidor, you will also need a humidifier to keep the tobacco from drying out and a hygrometer to measure the humidity inside the chest. These are available from The Woodworkers' Store as well.

How do I build it?

Enough about size and design. Ready for some routing? We're just about there, if you'll bear with me for one more page. First off, we need to select and prepare the wood for this project.

PREPARING THE MATERIALS

Before you make the first cut or even plane the boards, there's some important work to do.

SHOP-DRYING Bring the wood you intend to use for this chest into your shop and let it "shop-dry" for a week or more. During this time, the moisture content in the wood will adjust to the relative humidity in your shop. If you don't take the time to shop-dry it, the wood may be in motion when you cut it, and joints that fit perfectly on Monday may be nothing to crow about by Friday.

Don't think that just because you buy your wood locally or store it in a nearby barn it will be at the same moisture content as your shop. Not true — Jim and I found this out the hard way. We were building a tool chest (different from the one on page 7), and although we had enough cherry lying around the shop to make the drawers, we needed some larger stock for the case. So we went out to the storage barn just outside our shop, selected the lumber, brought it back inside, and cut it up. By the end of the week, the case parts, which were less than a foot wide, had shrunk so much that the drawers protruded ¼ inch from the case when they were closed. We had to rout out spaces in the plywood back so the drawer fronts would rest flush with the front of the case.

BUSTING UP THE LUMBER After the wood has shop dried, decide which parts you will make from which boards. Sketch the parts on the boards, label them, then cut the lumber into lengths and widths that you can handle easily. Old-timers I know call this *busting up* the lumber.

JOINTING AND PLANING Plane each piece to the thickness required. As designed, most of the chest is made from ½-inch-thick materials, while some of the drawer parts are ⅛ and ¼ inch thick and the lid parts are ⅝ inch thick. To make the parts as true as possible, joint one face of each board before planing it. Jim and I don't have a wide-bed jointer, so we can't do this for every part, but we do it for those narrow pieces where straightness and flatness are critical — such as the drawer parts and drawer guides in this chest.

PLANING FIGURED WOOD

Making a small box or chest is a great opportunity to use a piece of highly figured wood that you may have squirreled away. The box shape offers flat surfaces to display spectacular grain patterns. For example, to build this mule chest, Jim and I used an eye-popping piece of *quilted* maple. The quilted or "blistered" figure is thought to be due to a fungus that causes the wood to grow in dimples.

SHOP SAVVY ■ *Wrapping a Board around a Box*

When building a chest or a box, the corner joints look better when the wood grain and color match. To ensure that they do, pick a single board that's large enough to make all four sides, then "wrap" the board around the box. Cut the board into segments, then join the segments end to end in the same order and orientation that they were in the board.

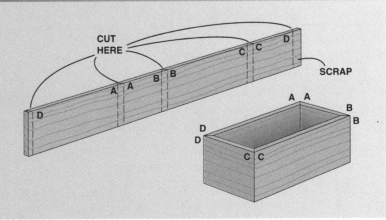

TRY THIS!

You can "stretch" a piece of figured wood and make it go farther by *resawing* it on a band saw. Our piece of quilted maple was about 2 board feet shy of what we needed to make the chest. But Jim split a portion of the board on the band saw to make the thin stock for the box bottoms and drawer parts.

Use your router as a surface planer on figured lumber — this prevents chipping and tear-out. You can also use this technique to flatten a wide board if you don't have a wide-bed jointer.

However spectacular, there is a drawback to using figured wood — it's difficult to plane. Because the grain direction in curly, burly, and quilted wood goes every which way, the planer knives sometimes dig in and tear out big chunks of wood.

There are two ways to get around this. If you have access to a *thickness sander,* you can have your figured stock sanded to the thicknesses needed. Or you can plane the lumber with your router.

Mount the router on an extended baseplate. Place the board you want to plane between two rails equal in height. Mount a wide straight bit in the router, and secure the board between the rails with wedges. Adjust the depth of cut so the bit cuts no more than ⅛ inch of stock on any one pass.

Move the router from side to side over the board, slowly drawing it along the rails. Because the bit attacks the wood from a different angle than planer knives, it is much less likely to tear or chip the stock.

The resulting surface will be perfectly flat. Clean up any steps or mill marks with a scraper or sander.

Once you have planed the lumber to the thicknesses you need, cut the parts to length and width. On our chest, the front of the chest and the drawer front are made from the same piece so the wood grain will appear continuous when the drawer is closed. To do this, I first cut the chest front piece about ½ inch longer and wider than specified in the Materials List. Then I ripped it into strips and cut the middle strip into three parts, as shown in

QUICK FIXTURE ■ *Router Planing Jig*

With the aid of this jig, you can use your router to surface small and medium-sized boards, up to 4 feet long and 13 inches wide. Make the extended base from ¼-inch clear acrylic plastic — this lets you see the work as you rout. Fasten braces along the length to stiffen it and stops at the ends to prevent it from sliding off the rails.

Make the base from ¾-inch plywood, and attach rails to the edges to support the router and the extended base above the work. To mount a board in the base, center it between the rails. Drive wedges between the rails and the edges of the board. For narrow boards, either move one of the rails or add spacers.

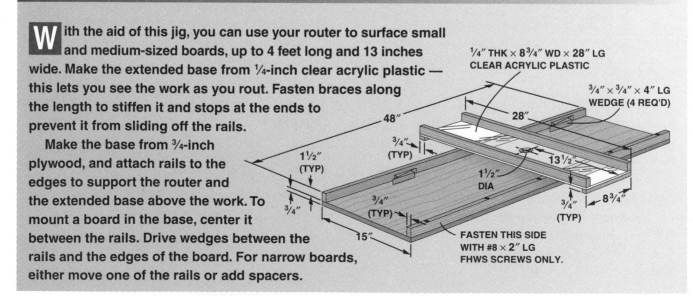

¼" THK × 8¾" WD × 28" LG CLEAR ACRYLIC PLASTIC

¾" × ¾" × 4" LG WEDGE (4 REQ'D)

48"

28"

¾" (TYP)

1½" (TYP)

13½"

1½" DIA

¾" (TYP)

¾" (TYP)

8¾"

¾"

15"

FASTEN THIS SIDE WITH #8 × 2" LG FHWS SCREWS ONLY.

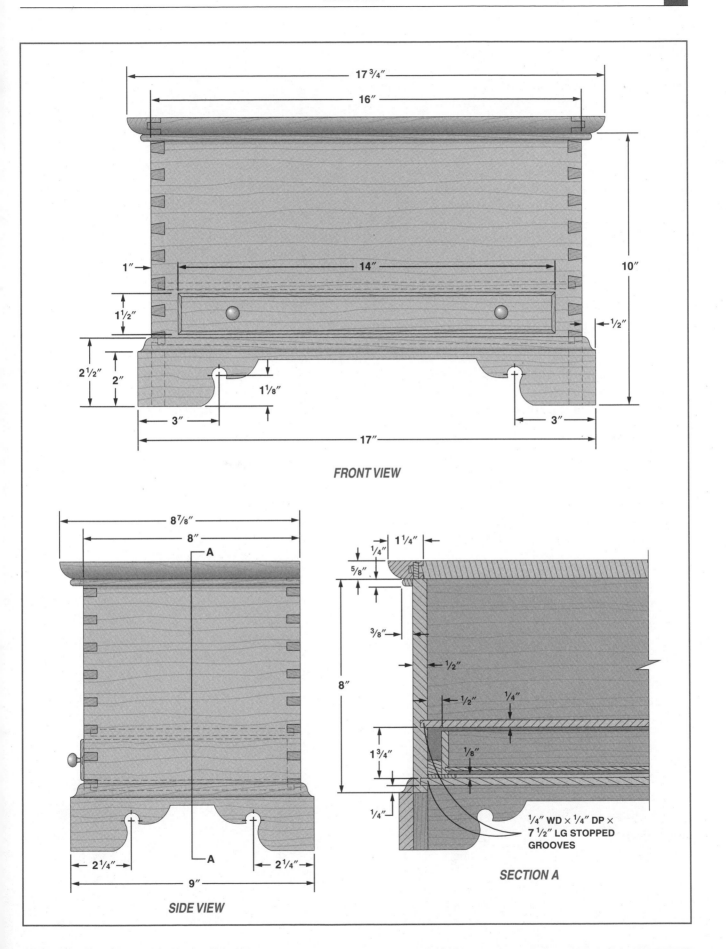

FRONT VIEW

SIDE VIEW

SECTION A

1/4" WD × 1/4" DP ×
7 1/2" LG STOPPED
GROOVES

the *Chest Front Assembly* diagram. Set the middle part aside for the drawer front, and glue the remaining four pieces back together to create the chest front. Once the glue dries, trim the chest front to size.

The opening in the completed chest front must be exactly the same size as the drawer front. For this to be so, you'll have to cheat the two small pieces toward the opening a fraction of an inch to make up for the saw kerfs. The grain won't be precisely continuous, but no one will ever know unless they examine the chest with a microscope.

MAKING THE BOX JOINERY

The first step in making the mule chest is to join the box parts — front, back, sides, till bottom, and chest bottom. When you do so, you must allow for the expansion and contraction of the wood with changes in the weather. Standard *box construction* provides for this movement. Join the front, back, and sides rigidly at the corners. As long as the grain

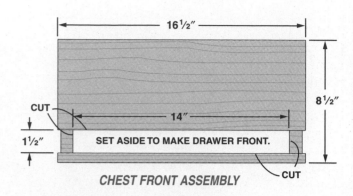

CHEST FRONT ASSEMBLY

runs lengthwise through the parts, they will move in unison. Common corner joints include miter, rabbet, lock, finger, through dovetails, and half-blind dovetails.

The wood grain in the bottoms, however, will always move perpendicular to some of the box parts, no matter how you orient the grain. So you must allow these parts to "float," free to expand and contract independently of the others. Common floating joints are groove, rabbet-and-groove, and tongue-and-groove.

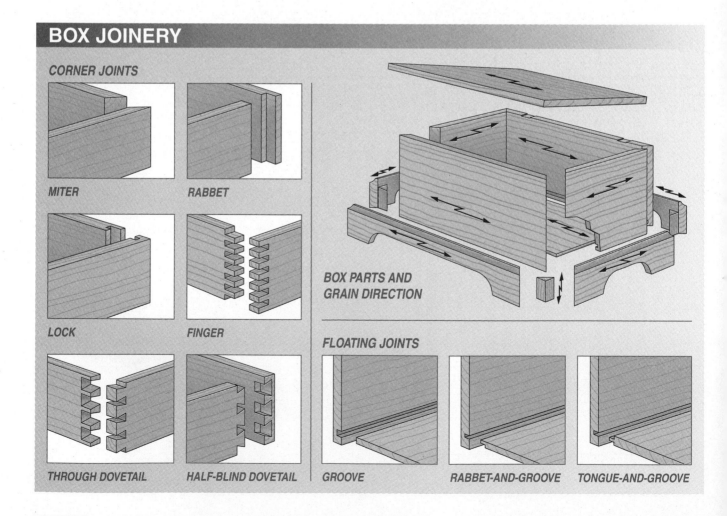

BOX JOINERY

CORNER JOINTS

MITER

RABBET

LOCK

FINGER

THROUGH DOVETAIL

HALF-BLIND DOVETAIL

BOX PARTS AND GRAIN DIRECTION

FLOATING JOINTS

GROOVE

RABBET-AND-GROOVE

TONGUE-AND-GROOVE

JOINING THE SIDES, FRONT, BACK, AND BOTTOM

On our mule chest, Jim and I decided to join the corners with traditional through dovetails. The till bottom and chest bottom float in grooves in the inside faces of the front, back, and sides, as shown in the *Box Joinery Layout*. You can make both joints with a router.

Rout the grooves first, but make them *stopped* grooves. That is, don't cut them from end to end — stop them just ¼ inch short of each end. If you cut them through, you will see the ends of the grooves in the assembled box.

Rout the grooves in box parts, guiding the router along a straightedge. Any straight board will do to guide the router, but the T-Square Guide makes it much easier to set up for the cuts. See page 15.

SHOP SAVVY

When joining box corners, turn the boards so the annual rings cup toward the outside of the assembly. Plain-sawn boards have a tendency to cup opposite the rings. If the rings cup in, gaps may develop at the corners.

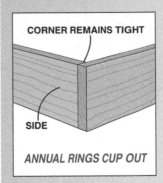
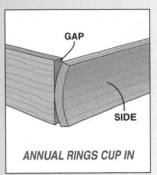

CORNER REMAINS TIGHT

SIDE

ANNUAL RINGS CUP OUT

GAP

SIDE

ANNUAL RINGS CUP IN

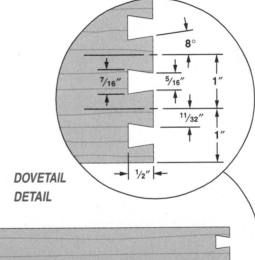

DOVETAIL
DETAIL

8°

7/16" 5/16" 1"

11/32" 1"

1/2"

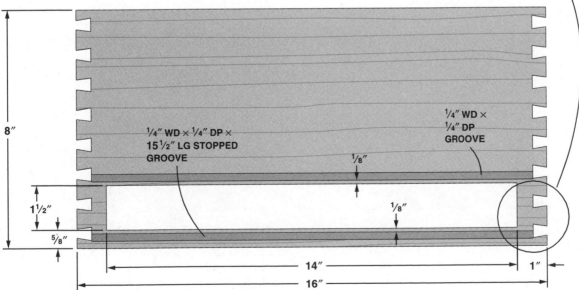

8"

¼" WD × ¼" DP × 15½" LG STOPPED GROOVE

¼" WD × ¼" DP GROOVE

⅛"

⅛"

1½"

⅝"

14"

1"

16"

BOX JOINERY LAYOUT

METHODS OF WORK ■ *Routing Rabbets, Dadoes, and Grooves*

For many woodworkers, a router is the tool of choice for making wood joints. It makes clean cuts, leaving smooth surfaces. This in turn results in better glue joints. The router is also extremely versatile. You can use it either hand-held or mounted in a table, depending on the size of the work and the type of joint you want to make. Furthermore, it gives you several options for making many common joints, especially rabbets, dadoes, and grooves.

Warning: For all of these operations, remember to cut *against* the rotation of the bit.

Look Here! For several helpful pro routing secrets, see page 29.

ROUTING RABBETS

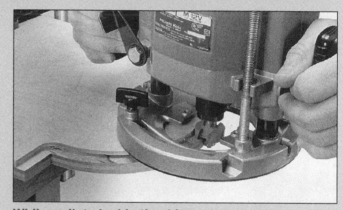

To make a rabbet on the edge or end of a board, use a straight bit *(left)* or a piloted rabbeting bit *(right)*. The piloted rabbeting bit has a post or ball-bearing that bears against the side of the work to guide the cut. Many come with several sizes of bearings to vary the width of the rabbet.

While a piloted rabbeting bit can be used to rout straight edges, it's especially useful for cutting rabbets along the edges of curved workpieces. The bearing follows the curved edge precisely. Adjust the depth of the rabbet by changing the depth of cut and the width of the rabbet by changing bearings. The smaller the bearing, the wider the rabbet.

When rabbeting a straight surface with a hand-held router, consider a straight bit and an edge guide. Adjust the width of the rabbet by changing the position of the guide. As you rout, keep the guide firmly against the work. This setup is especially useful for long cuts and large workpieces.

For small and medium-sized work, a table-mounted router is more appropriate. Mount a straight bit in the router, and use the fence to guide the work. Adjust the width of the rabbet by changing the position of the fence. Warning: Always "bury" the unused portion of the router bit in the fence — the fence will serve as a guard.

ROUTING STRAIGHT DADOES AND GROOVES

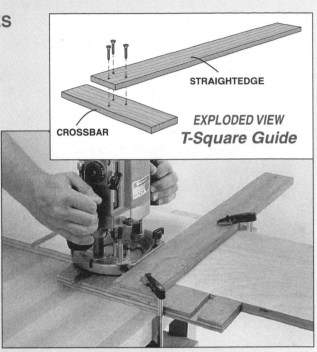

STRAIGHTEDGE

CROSSBAR

EXPLODED VIEW
T-Square Guide

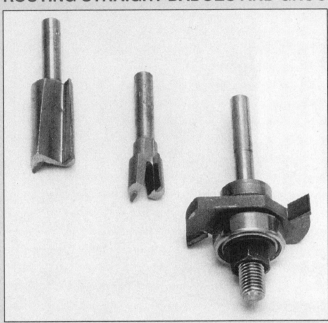

To make dadoes and grooves, use a straight bit *(left),* a mortising bit *(middle),* or a slot cutter *(right).* While straight bits and mortising bits can cut recesses of almost any size anywhere on a board, slot cutters are designed to cut narrow recesses along the edge of a workpiece.

One of the simplest ways to rout precise dadoes and grooves with a hand-held router is to clamp a straightedge to the work and guide the router along it. Not only does a shop-made T-square guide the router, its crossbar helps to square the straightedge to the edge of the board.

You can also use a dado and rabbet jig (see page 17) with a hand-held router. This is especially handy when making dadoes and rabbets across the width of long boards, such as cabinet sides or shelving supports. The straightedge doubles as a guide and a clamp. For plans, see page 17.

When routing dadoes and grooves on a router table, use the fence to guide the work. **Warning: Even though the bit doesn't cut completely through the wood when you're making these joints, never allow your hand to pass over the bit. If necessary, use a push block to feed the work.**

(continued)

METHODS OF WORK ■ *Routing Rabbets, Dadoes, and Grooves* — CONTINUED

ROUTING CURVED GROOVES

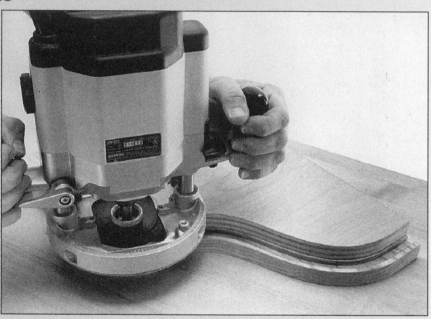

To rout a curved groove, make a curved template to guide the router. Attach a guide collar to the base of the router, and insert a straight bit through the collar. As you rout, keep the collar pressed firmly against the edge of the template.

MAKING STOPPED CUTS

Often, you need to make *stopped* rabbets, dadoes and grooves — cuts that stop before you cut through the edge or end of a board. If you're using a hand-held router and can clearly see the cut, you can simply stop the cut at a mark. But when you can't see the cut, or precision is important, use a stop to halt the cut. In this operation, Jim has clamped a stop next to the dado and rabbet jig to stop the router when the bit is just ½ inch from the front edge of the workpiece.

You can also use a stop on a router table, clamping it to the table or the fence. Or, mark the stopped end of the cut on a surface of the board that will be visible during the operation. Then mark the diameter of the bit on a piece of tape affixed to the fence or table. Halt the cut when the proper mark on the board lines up with the desired tape mark.

QUICK FIXTURE ▪ *Dado-and-Rabbet Jig*

The clamp bar on this fixture serves as both a clamp and a guide. Slide the work between the bar and the base, then tighten the knobs. The clamp bar locks the work in position. A guide in the base helps square the board to the clamp bar. With the work in position, rout the dado or rabbet, guiding the router along the bar. When you've completed the cut, loosen the knobs. A pair of compression springs automatically raise the bar.

You can make the base from plywood, but the clamp bar should be a strong hardwood, such as maple, oak, or ash, to keep from bending under pressure. You can make this jig any size; but if you make the clamp bar much longer than shown, put a slight crown on the underside ($\frac{1}{32}$ to $\frac{1}{16}$ inch). This will help distribute the pressure more evenly along the length of the bar when it's tightened down.

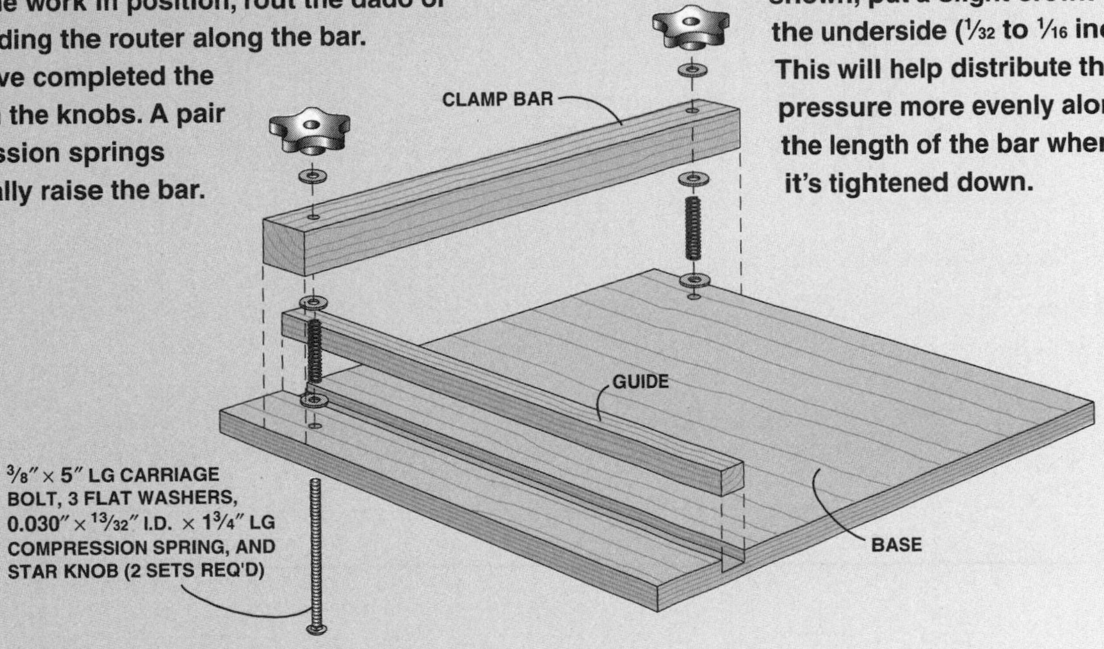

CLAMP BAR

GUIDE

BASE

$\frac{3}{8}$" × 5" LG CARRIAGE BOLT, 3 FLAT WASHERS, 0.030" × $\frac{13}{32}$" I.D. × $1\frac{3}{4}$" LG COMPRESSION SPRING, AND STAR KNOB (2 SETS REQ'D)

EXPLODED VIEW

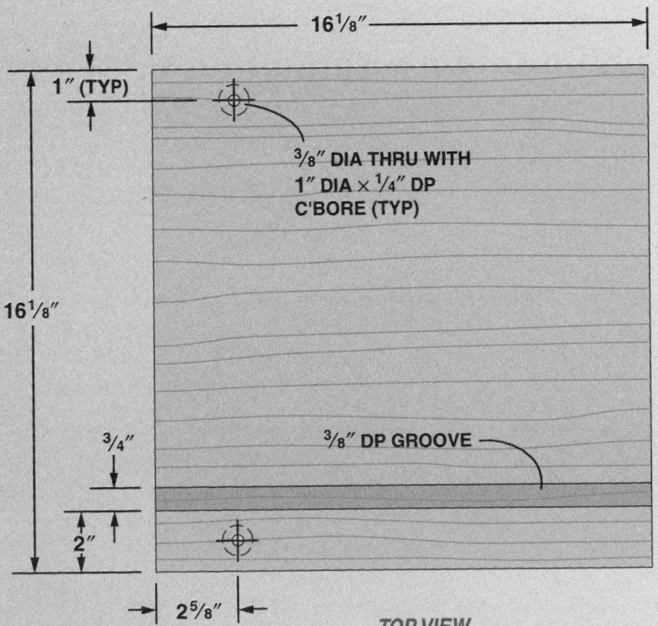

16$\frac{1}{8}$"

1" (TYP)

$\frac{3}{8}$" DIA THRU WITH 1" DIA × $\frac{1}{4}$" DP C'BORE (TYP)

16$\frac{1}{8}$"

$\frac{3}{4}$"

$\frac{3}{8}$" DP GROOVE

2"

2$\frac{5}{8}$"

TOP VIEW
BASE

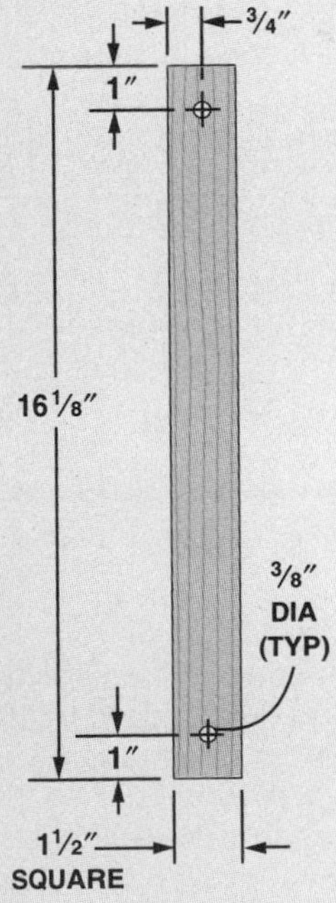

$\frac{3}{4}$"

1"

16$\frac{1}{8}$"

$\frac{3}{8}$" DIA (TYP)

1"

1$\frac{1}{2}$" SQUARE

TOP VIEW
CLAMP BAR

ROUTING THROUGH DOVETAILS

Once you've made the grooves, rout the dovetails that join the corners of the chest. Rout the tails in the front and back, and the pins in the sides.

Making through dovetails is one of those operations where the router really shines, making short work of an otherwise tedious job. It's a *pattern-routing* operation — you follow a template. There are several dovetail templates on the market, and they all work pretty much the same way. The fixtures mount two "combs" — one for the tails and the other for the pins. With a guide collar mounted to the base of the router, these templates guide the router as you cut. Create the tails with a dovetail bit, and the pins with a straight bit.

If you don't have a dovetail fixture, no matter. You can easily make your own, as I'll show you in the next few pages.

Look Here! For more information on pattern routing, see page 83.

METHODS OF WORK ■ *Routing Through Dovetails*

WITH A COMMERCIAL JIG

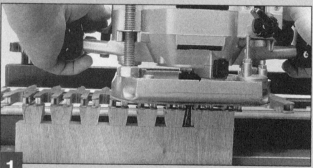

1 **To rout a through dovetail joint,** start with the tails. Mount the tail comb over the end of the board that you want to rout, and mount a guide collar and a dovetail bit in the router. Following the comb with the collar, cut the tails in the board.

2 **Mount the pin comb** over the end of the adjoining board, and mount a straight bit in the router. Rout the pins, following the comb with the collar. **Alert! The direction in which the boards face as you rout them is important. Most fixtures are made so you rout the tails with the inside surface facing out and the pins with the outside surface facing out.**

WITH A SHOP-MADE JIG

1 **The procedure for routing dovetails** with our shop-made template is similar. Mount the tail comb over the work, and rout the tails with a dovetail bit. Note that I'm using the Dado-and-Rabbet Jig (page 17) to hold the board as I work.

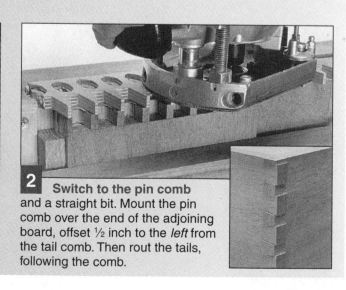

2 **Switch to the pin comb** and a straight bit. Mount the pin comb over the end of the adjoining board, offset ½ inch to the *left* from the tail comb. Then rout the tails, following the comb.

QUICK FIXTURE ■ *Through Dovetail Template*

Although a dovetail template must be precise, it's nothing you can't make in your own shop with a cooperative table saw. The trick is not to cut out the comb but to make the individual *teeth* all precisely the same, then string them together on a threaded rod.

The teeth are all 1 inch wide and are designed to cut tails and pins on 1-inch centers, similar to the tails shown in the *Dovetail Detail* on page 13. We did this to make it easier to plan your projects. The joints will look best if the boards you join are a *whole number* of inches wide — 3, 4, 5, 6, and so on.

String the identical teeth together on threaded rods to make the combs. (One advantage of making your own dovetail jig is that you can make the combs any length you need — just add or subtract teeth as required.)

Make a simple bracket to mount the combs — a base and a back braced with ribs. To hold the work, fasten the Dado-and-Rabbet Jig (page 17) to the back. Alert! The combs are mounted to the top edge of the back, but *not* in the same location. The pin comb must be secured ½ inch to the left of the tail comb.

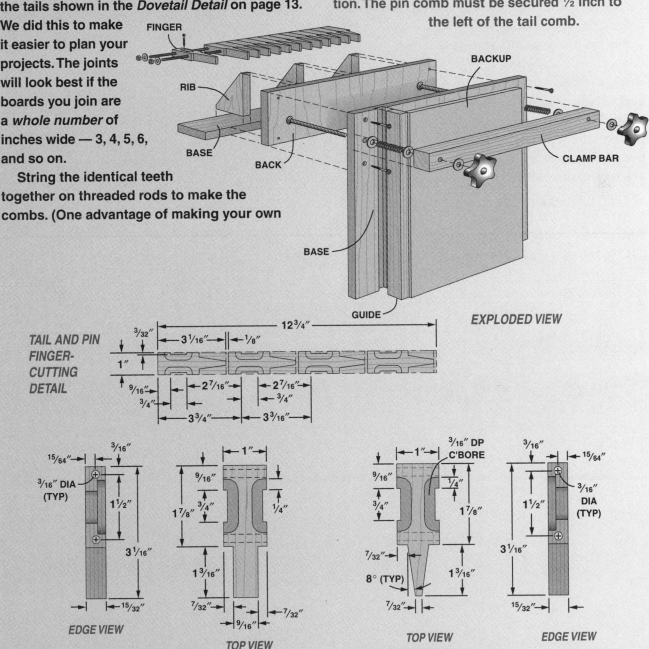

(continued)

QUICK FIXTURE Through Dovetail Template — CONTINUED

Also, the guide in this jig is wider than the one shown for cutting dadoes. It must protrude beyond the backup — a disposable scrap of wood attached to the jig to back up the work and prevent it from tearing out when the router exits the cut. Jim and I stick the backup to the base of the Dado-and-Rabbet Jig with double-faced carpet tape. This makes it easy to replace when it becomes chewed up.

Fasten the combs to the top edge of the back with screws — one screw every three or four teeth. Drive the screws through the notches in the edges of the teeth. These notches form slots in the assembled combs that allow you to adjust the positions of the combs forward and back.

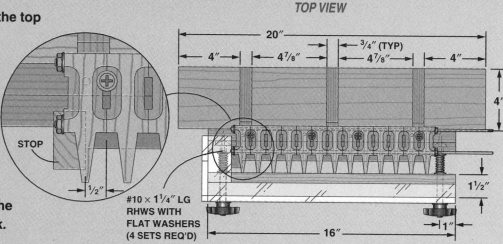

STOP

1"

TAIL FINGER SETUP
TOP VIEW

STOP

1/2"

#10 × 1¹/₄" LG
RHWS WITH
FLAT WASHERS
(4 SETS REQ'D)

20"

4"   4⁷/₈"   ³/₄" (TYP)   4⁷/₈"   4"

4"

1¹/₂"

16"   1"

PIN FINGER SETUP
TOP VIEW

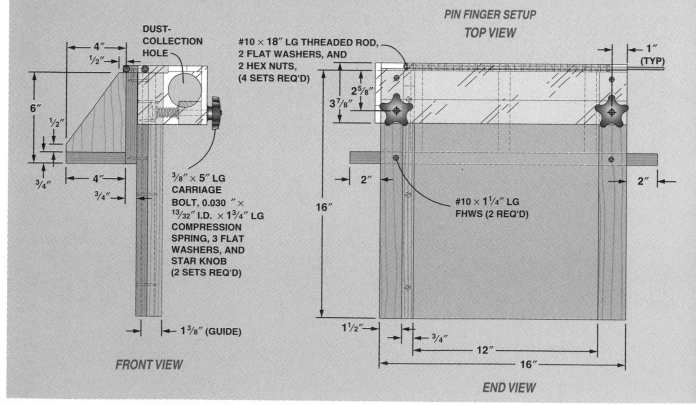

DUST-COLLECTION HOLE

4"

1/2"

6"

1/2"

3/4"

4"

3/4"

1³/₈" (GUIDE)

³/₈" × 5" LG CARRIAGE BOLT, 0.030 " × ¹³/₃₂" I.D. × 1³/₄" LG COMPRESSION SPRING, 3 FLAT WASHERS, AND STAR KNOB (2 SETS REQ'D)

FRONT VIEW

#10 × 18" LG THREADED ROD, 2 FLAT WASHERS, AND 2 HEX NUTS, (4 SETS REQ'D)

1" (TYP)

2⁵/₈"

3⁷/₈"

16"

2"

2"

#10 × 1¹/₄" LG FHWS (2 REQ'D)

1¹/₂"   ³/₄"

12"

16"

END VIEW

MAKING THE TEETH

You can make the teeth of the comb with the aid of a table saw, drill press, and router table. It's important that each of the teeth are identical, so make sure all your tools are properly aligned and adjusted. Take your time as you work. Feeding work too quickly over a saw blade may cause the blade to vibrate, making the cut uneven. Feeding a router bit too fast may cause it to wander off its mark.

Jim and I found out the hard way that it's also a good idea to make six more teeth than you think you'll need and to rip extra stock and set it aside in case you want to make more teeth in the future.

The most critical measurement in this operation is the width of the teeth — they must all be *exactly* the same. (In fact, it's more important that they're all the same width than it is that they're 1 inch wide.) It's difficult to duplicate the same rip setup with the precision needed, so make a few extra strips while you're at it.

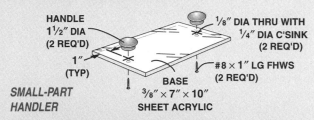

HANDLE
1½" DIA
(2 REQ'D)

1"
(TYP)

⅛" DIA THRU WITH
¼" DIA C'SINK
(2 REQ'D)

#8 × 1" LG FHWS
(2 REQ'D)

SMALL-PART
HANDLER

BASE
⅜" × 7" × 10"
SHEET ACRYLIC

1 **Rip 1-inch-wide, 12½-inch-long strips** from ½-inch-thick cabinet-grade plywood. Discard any strip with voids in the plies. Each strip will make four teeth. Lay out the teeth, and cut the notches in the edges by running the strips over a dado cutter (on a table saw) or a straight bit (on a router table).

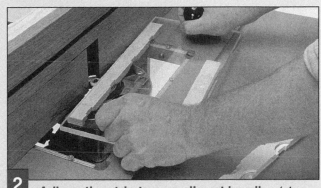

2 **Adhere the strip to a small-part handler** *(shown in drawing above)* with carpet tape. Using a rabbeting bit in a table-mounted router, cut a rabbet around the top edges of the notches. When the teeth are strung together, these rabbets will become recesses for the heads of the screws that hold the combs to the bracket.

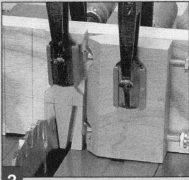

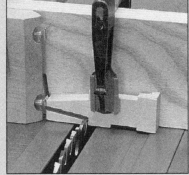

3 **On a table saw,** cut each strip into individual teeth. Cut the cheeks, then the shoulders of each tooth. Use a miter gauge extension and a stop block to hold and position the teeth as you cut them. When cutting the pin teeth, angle the blade at 8 degrees to match the slope of the dovetail bit you'll use to rout the joint.

4 **Drill holes in the edges** of the teeth where you will insert the threaded rods. Use a fence and stop block for added precision.

(continued)

QUICK FIXTURE ■ *Through Dovetail Template* — CONTINUED

MAKING AND TESTING THE COMBS

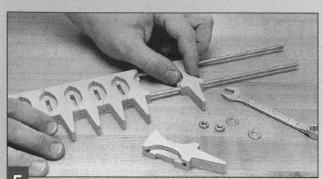

5 String the teeth together on threaded rods to make a tail comb and pin comb. Each comb should have the same number of teeth. And the length of each comb, after you tighten the nuts that secure the teeth, should be identical. If one comb is slightly longer than the other, lengthen the short comb by adding paper or masking tape shims between the teeth.

RESOURCES

You can purchase the guide collar (#BTG-006), the dovetail bit (#818-129), and the straight bit (#811-081) from Jesada Tools, 310 Mears Boulevard, Oldsmar, FL 34677.

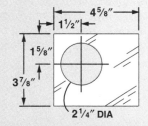

6 Install a $^7/_{16}$-inch-O.D. guide collar in the base of your router. Make a single dovetail joint to test the combs — tails first, using a $^1/_2$-inch-diameter, $^{13}/_{16}$-inch-long 8-degree dovetail bit. Then make the pins with a $^5/_{16}$-inch-diameter, 1-inch-long straight bit. Both bits must have $^1/_4$-inch-diameter shanks. If the joint is too tight, move the pin comb back slightly to reduce the size of the pins. If it's too loose, move the pin comb forward to increase the pin size.

QUICK FIXTURE ■ *Dovetail Dust Collector*

Routing dovetails can be a messy job. The router removes a lot of stock between the pins and tails. And if you want to watch the cuts as they progress, as most craftsmen do, the machine spits the dust right in your face. Consequently, I wear a face shield and full dust armor when making these joints.

In making this jig, however, Jim came up with a better solution — a dust collector that mounts in front of the clamp bar and allows you to connect a vacuum hose to the jig so you can suck up the wood chips as you make them.

This collector has another advantage — it helps balance the router on the combs and prevents it from tipping forward. This increases the ease and accuracy of the operation.

As drawn here, the collector fits our dovetail jig. But you can easily adapt the design to work with most commercial fixtures.

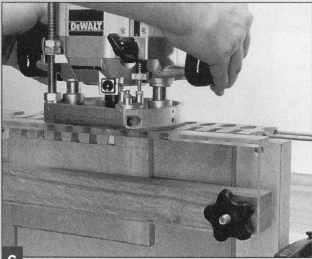

END LAYOUT (INSIDE VIEW)

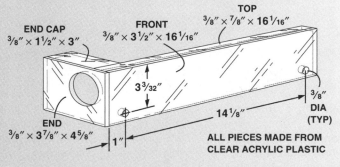

END CAP
$^3/_8$" × $1^1/_2$" × 3"

FRONT
$^3/_8$" × $3^1/_2$" × $16^1/_{16}$"

TOP
$^3/_8$" × $^7/_8$" × $16^1/_{16}$"

END
$^3/_8$" × $3^7/_8$" × $4^5/_8$"

ALL PIECES MADE FROM CLEAR ACRYLIC PLASTIC

NO PROBLEM ■ *Fixing Sloppy Dovetails*

Even with a first-class dovetail jig, the router sometimes slips, leaving a gap between a pin and a tail. No problem. With a little patience, you can disguise these gaps so they're almost impossible to detect.

1 **The first step,** believe it or not, is to make the gap worse. Using a dovetail saw or a Japanese *dozuki* saw, cut along the gaping joint between the tail and the pin. This widens the gap to a consistent width, making it easier to fill.

2 **From the scraps of wood** left over from the project, cut a sliver of wood to fill the expanded gap. Glue the sliver in the gap. When in place, the grain direction, pattern, and color must match either the adjoining pin or the adjoining tail as closely as possible.

3 **After the glue dries,** sand the protruding parts of the patch flush with the surrounding surfaces. If you made a good match, you won't be able to see the patch with just a casual inspection.

ASSEMBLING THE BOX

"Dry" assemble the chest — that is, assemble the parts *without* glue — to check the fit of the joints. When you're satisfied that the front, back, sides, and bottoms all fit together properly and the assembly is square, finish sand the parts and apply a finish to those surfaces that will end up inside the drawer cavity in the assembled chest. (They will be almost impossible to reach after assembly.)

Apply glue to the tails and pins, and assemble the chest. *Don't* put any glue in the grooves. Remember, the bottoms must be allowed to float.

When gluing up the chest parts, apply the clamps in a crisscross pattern to put even pressure on all sides. Protect the corners with strips of wood or *cauls.* To keep from fumbling with the cauls, stick them to the wood surfaces with tabs of double-faced carpet tape.

TRY THIS!

To prevent glue squeeze-out from hardening on the inside surfaces of the box, mask off the areas near the inside corners with tape during dry assembly. After final assembly, let the glue dry, then peel off the tape and the squeeze-out.

MAKING A FRAME BASE The chest sits on a frame base — a decorative frame, mitered at the corners. Rout an ogee shape in the top edges of the frame parts, then cut the miters, fitting the frame around the assembled chest. Cut the feet profiles, as shown in the *Foot Layout/Side View* and *Foot Layout/Front View.*

Assemble the base frame parts with glue, reinforcing the corners with glue blocks. Remember, the case rests on these blocks. The tops of the blocks must all be even, ½ inch from the top edge of the molded frame parts.

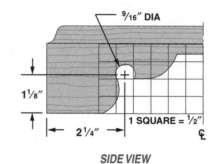

SIDE VIEW

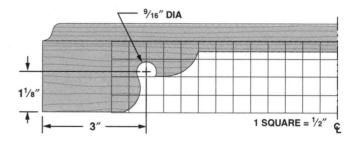

FRONT VIEW
FOOT LAYOUT

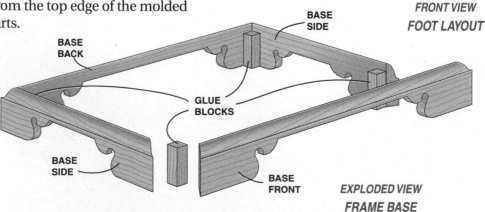

EXPLODED VIEW
FRAME BASE

MAKING A BREADBOARD LID

The "breadboard" ends on the lid prevent the lid from cupping. This was a common device employed by old-time cabinetmakers to prevent wide boards from cupping. It does the job, but it presents another problem. The wood grain in the breadboards is perpendicular to the grain in the lid. If you glue the breadboards in place, they eventually will cause the lid to split.

David T. Smith, a master craftsman who makes American Country furniture, showed me his solution to the breadboard dilemma, and I've used it ever since. The breadboards are attached to the lid with a tongue-and-groove joint and are glued to the lid only at the middle (in an area less than 2 inches wide). The ends are *pinned,* and the pins are driven through slots in the tongues. In essence, the back and the front of the lid float in the breadboards, free to expand and contract.

On a router table, cut tongues on the ends of the lids and matching grooves in the edges of the breadboards. Dry assemble the breadboards and the lid. Working from the underside, drill peg holes through the breadboards and the tongues on the lid where shown in the *Breadboard Lid/Bottom View.* Do not drill through to the top surface. Using a rat-tail file, widen the outboard holes in the lid to create slots, as shown in the *Pinned Joint Detail.*

Put spots of glue in the breadboard grooves near the center, but nowhere else. Clamp the breadboards to the lid. Using a toothpick to apply the glue carefully, secure the pegs in their holes but not in the slots.

Rout the narrow slots in the breadboard ends with a slot cutter. You can make sure the slots are perfectly centered in the edge of the work by making two passes past the bit. On the second pass, flip the work face for face.

To create matching tongues in the lid, rout a rabbet in one face, then turn the board over and cut a second rabbet. Use a large, square scrap to help feed the work and keep it properly aligned to the bit to prevent tear-out when the bit exits the cut. You can use a slot cutter for this operation, too.

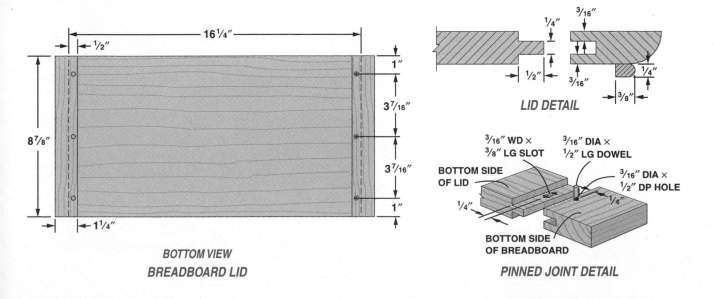

BOTTOM VIEW
BREADBOARD LID

LID DETAIL

PINNED JOINT DETAIL

HINGING THE LID ON THE BOX

The lid is hinged to the chest with special "quadrant hinges," which serve as both hinges and lid supports. This hardware requires special mortises. Not only must you make a recess for the leaves, you must also create deep sockets to hold the quadrants when the lid is closed.

First, lay out the position of the hinges on the sides and back of the chest. Place the lid on the chest. Using a small square, transfer the marks from the back of the chest to the back edge of the lid, then lay out the hinge mortises on the lid.

Routing the hinge mortises in the lid is straightforward — just make shallow L-shaped mortises. Use a straightedge to guide the router, or a fixture like the T-Square Guide (see page 15).

Creating the mortises and recesses in the chest is more of a challenge. First, you must balance the router on the thin edge of the sides. An extended base straddling the front, back, and sides for maximum support solves that problem. Then you must guide the router in a straight line and stop it when the mortise is the desired length. To do this, affix a fence with stops to the bottom of the extended base and affix a guide to the side of the chest. Secure both fixtures with double-faced carpet tape.

Rout the mortise first, then switch to a narrower bit. Using the same setup, rout a recess for the quadrant.

Install the hinges and check the movement of the lid. If the action seems to hang up at any point, or the lid won't close all the way, you may have to rout the recesses a little deeper. After installing the hinges, rout a small bead molding as shown in the *Lid Detail* on page 25. Apply it to the underside of the lid, near the front and side edges.

Look Here! For more information on routing molded shapes, see page 67.

A quadrant hinge incorporates both a hinge and a lid support. The quadrant disappears into a recess in the side of the chest when the lid is closed.

To rout the mortises in the chest for the quadrant hinges, mount the router on an extended base to help balance it. Attach a fence (to guide the router) and stops (to halt the cut) to the bottom of the extended base. Attach a guide to the box side to keep the router aligned. As you rout, keep the fence pressed against the side of the chest.

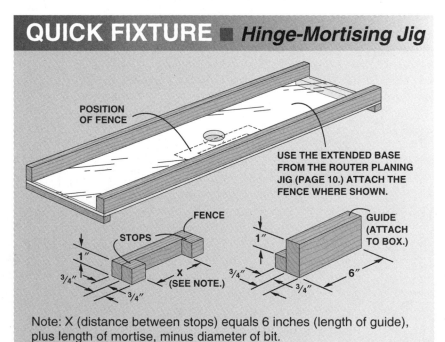

QUICK FIXTURE ■ *Hinge-Mortising Jig*

POSITION OF FENCE

USE THE EXTENDED BASE FROM THE ROUTER PLANING JIG (PAGE 10.) ATTACH THE FENCE WHERE SHOWN.

FENCE

STOPS

1"

3/4"

3/4"

X (SEE NOTE.)

1"

3/4"

3/4"

6"

GUIDE (ATTACH TO BOX.)

Note: X (distance between stops) equals 6 inches (length of guide), plus length of mortise, minus diameter of bit.

MAKING THE DRAWER

The drawer in the mule chest is just another box construction — front, back, and sides rigidly joined at the corners with a floating bottom. The difference is the joinery. The front corners of the drawer are joined with lock joints. These joints are "blind" at the front so they can't be seen when the drawer is closed. The back corners are joined with rabbets and dadoes. And the drawer bottom floats in grooves. As you might expect, all of these joints can be made with a router.

The drawer front is trimmed with a decorative *cock bead*. This was an elegant fix for an unexpected problem. When Jim cut the drawer front free from the chest front, it bowed from internal tensions. We thought the piece was ruined — if we jointed it straight again, it would be too small to fit the drawer opening. After much weeping and wailing and gnashing of teeth, we suddenly remembered our design history — cock beads! These were used in the eighteenth and early nineteenth centuries to decorate the edges of doors and drawers.

We could use them to disguise the patches we needed to add to the drawer front! We did, and we liked the results so well that we decided we should have designed the chest this way in the first place.

Cock beads are probably the only decorative shapes in this book that you *can't* make efficiently

To use a scratch bead, simply push it along the wood, pressing down lightly. (Too much pressure will ruin the cut.) Each pass will remove a little more stock, and after several passes, the shape will emerge.

with a router. There are bits that will do the job for you, but it's just as easy to make a simple fixture called a *scratch bead* and scrape the shape in the edge of a 1/8-inch-thick board. After scraping the bead shape, rip the shaped edge from the board. Continue until you have made enough beading strips to apply around the perimeter of the drawer front.

After assembling the drawer, cut a rabbet around the perimeter of the drawer front, as shown in the *Cock Bead Profile*. Glue the cock bead in the rabbets, mitering the adjoining ends.

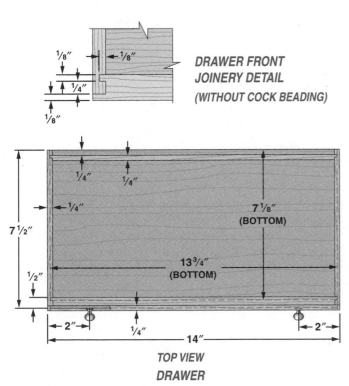

DRAWER FRONT
JOINERY DETAIL
(WITHOUT COCK BEADING)

1/8″   1/8″
1/4″
1/8″

7 1/2″

1/4″   1/4″

1/4″

7 1/8″
(BOTTOM)

1/2″

13 3/4″
(BOTTOM)

2″   1/4″   2″
14″

TOP VIEW
DRAWER

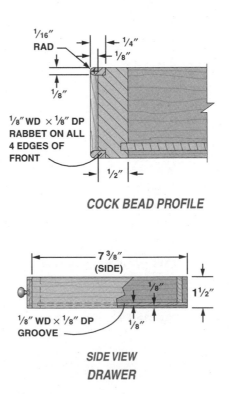

1/16″ RAD   1/4″
1/8″

1/8″

1/8″ WD × 1/8″ DP
RABBET ON ALL
4 EDGES OF
FRONT

1/2″

COCK BEAD PROFILE

7 3/8″
(SIDE)

1/8″

1 1/2″

1/8″ WD × 1/8″ DP
GROOVE   1/8″

SIDE VIEW
DRAWER

METHODS OF WORK ▪ *Making Lock Joints*

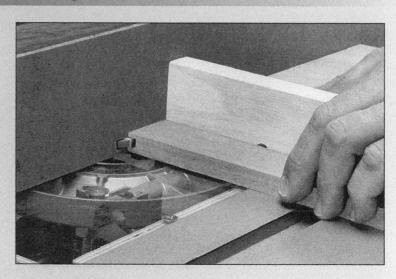

1   To make the lock joints that join the front corners of the drawer, first rout ¼-inch-wide grooves in the ends of the drawer front. Use a ¼-inch slot cutter to make the cut. Guide the work along the fence, feeding it with a square scrap of wood or plywood.

2   Each groove will create two tongues. Use the same slot cutter to trim the inside tongues so they're ⅛ inch long.

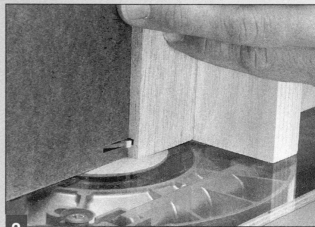

3   Using a ⅛-inch slot cutter, cut a ⅛-inch dado near the front ends of the sides. These dadoes must fit the short tenons on the drawer front.

QUICK FIXTURE ▪ *Scratch Bead*

To make the scratch bead, cut a notch in a scrap of hardwood. The notch helps guide the jig along the edge of the stock.

    Fashion a scraper blade from a segment of a used hacksaw blade, grinding or filing the round shape of the bead. Secure the blade to the wood scrap with roundhead screws so the rounded shape rests over the notch.

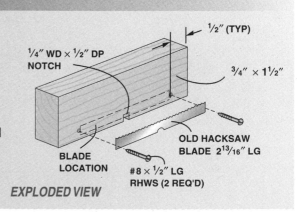

¼" WD × ½" DP NOTCH

½" (TYP)

¾" × 1½"

BLADE LOCATION

OLD HACKSAW BLADE 2¹³/₁₆" LG

#8 × ½" LG RHWS (2 REQ'D)

EXPLODED VIEW

SHOP SAVVY ■ *Pro Routing Secrets*

Whether you're new to routing or an old hand, you'll want to review this quick list of routing tips. These are the little things that make the difference between professional results and those that are less so.

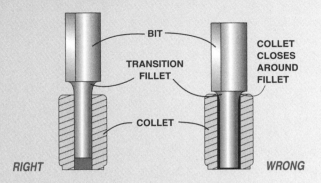

RIGHT   *WRONG*

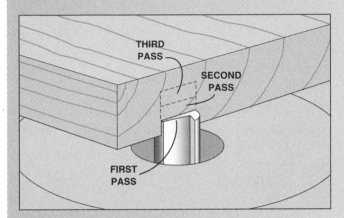

MOUNT THE BIT SECURELY

And this doesn't mean that you should overtighten the collet. For the bit to be secure, both the collet and the bit shank must be clean and smooth — free of sawdust and burrs. And be careful not to insert the bit so far into the collet that it closes around the fillet (the carved area between the shank and the flutes).

TAKE SMALL BITES

If you try to remove too much stock in one pass, the bit will vibrate and overheat, leaving a rough surface and burn marks. For deep cuts, remove 1/8 inch or less per pass in hardwoods, 1/4 inch or less in softwoods.

KEEP MOVING

Feed the router or the work steadily as you cut. If you pause or move too slowly, the bit will burn the wood.

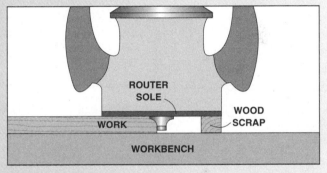

GUIDE THE ROUTER

Or the work, when using a router table. It's never a good idea to rout freehand. Use an edge guide, pilot bearing, guide collar, straightedge, fence, or template to provide the guidance needed.

BALANCE THE ROUTER

Routers are top-heavy. When routing a small workpiece or routing the edge of a large one, it may be difficult to balance the tool. Use an extended base or an offset base to help balance. You can also attach a wood scrap to the router sole or the bench to support the portion of the router base that overhangs the work.

CUT AGAINST THE BIT ROTATION

Always know which way the bit revolves: clockwise when using a hand-held router, counterclockwise when it's mounted in a table. Feed the router or the work in the opposite direction. If you cut with the rotation, the router tends to "run" or pull away from you or snatch the work out of your hands.

On those rare occasions when you absolutely must "back rout," as cutting with the rotation is called, take extremely small bites and hold the router or the work firmly.

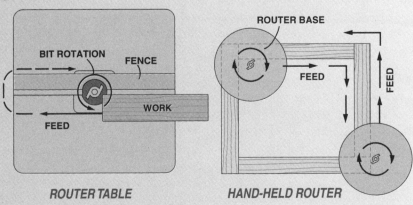

ROUTER TABLE   *HAND-HELD ROUTER*

Writing Table

In this chapter...

PRACTICAL KNOW-HOW

Joining Legs and Aprons	37
Routing a Thumbnail Edge	43
Routing Half-Blind Dovetails	44

JIGS AND FIXTURES

Mortising Template	39
Router Table Tenoning Jig	40
Fixed Calipers	42
Trammel Jig	49

SHOP SOLUTIONS

Squaring a Table Leg	35
Routing Mortises and Tenons	38
Routing Round Table Tops	46
Routing Oval Table Tops	47
Scooping a Piecrust Top	48

This classy little table neatly demonstrates how you can use a router to create the granddaddy of all woodworking joinery, the mortise-and-tenon joint. In fact, it's a good example of several types of router joinery.

The major parts of the structure — the legs and aprons — are joined with routed mortises and tenons. Additionally, the drawer guides are mortised into the inside surfaces of the front and back aprons. The drawer is joined with half-blind dovetails at the front corners and rabbet-and-dado joints at the back corners, and the bottom rests in grooves; these joints are all routed. Even the slots in the cleats that hold the table top to the aprons and allow it to expand and contract are created with a router.

Before we dive into some more routing techniques, however, we need to talk a little about the table itself.

What size should it be?

The writing table falls under the general category of *occasional and specialty tables* — tables designed for special purposes or occasions. These are usually relatively small pieces, such as a side table, a coffee table, and a candle stand. But they can be much larger, depending on the occasion. A sideboard or huntboard, for example, can be quite large and imposing.

The overall size — height, length, and depth — depends on how and where the table will be used. A side table is only 20 inches high, on average, because that's a comfortable height to hold a book, a drink, or the television remote, when you're seated on a couch or easy chair. Sideboards are usually counter height (36 inches) so you can stand and serve food from them.

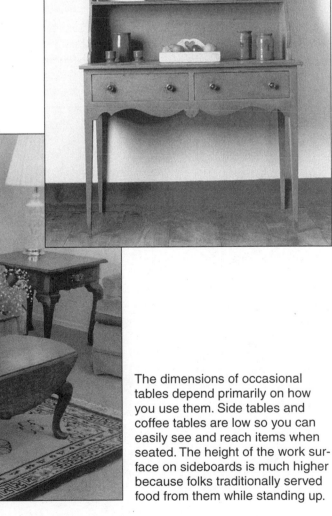

The dimensions of occasional tables depend primarily on how you use them. Side tables and coffee tables are low so you can easily see and reach items when seated. The height of the work surface on sideboards is much higher because folks traditionally served food from them while standing up.

The writing table is 27 inches high because that's a comfortable height at which to sit and write. Actually, if I really wanted it for *writing* — putting a pen to paper — I might have made it an inch or two higher. But I wanted it to support a laptop computer, and I like the keyboard fairly low.

Which brings us to the next consideration when designing a table. Will the table be used primarily by one or by two people? Will it be used by people whose body size is somewhat different from the body size of ordinary adults (such as children or professional basketball players)? You may want to adjust the standard dimensions of the table to better fit the people who will use it.

Take a look at the chart of *Standard Sizes for Occasional and Specialty Tables* and the information on *Table Ergonomics*. These will help you figure a general size for your table. Then fine-tune the dimensions according to your specific needs.

TRY THIS!

Unsure what size to make a table? There's nothing like a mock-up to help you fine-tune a design. When I designed this writing table, I set an old work-bench top across two saw-horses and began to peck away at my laptop computer. I experimented with different heights, raising and lowering the surface with shims until I found the most comfortable height.

STANDARD SIZES FOR OCCASIONAL AND SPECIALTY TABLES

TYPE	HEIGHT	LENGTH	DEPTH
Candlestand	24"–32"	15"–24"	15"–24"
Child's Table	20"–22"	26"–30"	18"–22"
Coffee Table	15"–18"	30"–60"	22"–30"
Computer Table	25"–28"	36"–60"	22"–30"
Drawing Table	32"–44"	31"–72"	23"–44"
Dressing Table	29"–30"	40"–48"	18"–22"
End Table	18"–24"	18"–24"	18"–24"
Game Table	28"–30"	30"–32"	30"–32"
Nightstand	24"–30"	18"–20"	18"–20"
Sideboard	34"–36"	23"–24"	30"–72"
Side Table	18"–24"	24"–28"	18"–20"
Writing Table	27"–30"	36"–42"	24"–30"

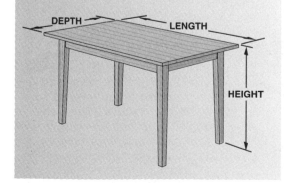

SHOP SAVVY ■ *Table Ergonomics*

When you design a table for working, writing, or some other activity, not only do you want the table top to rest at a comfortable height, you must also provide adequate reach, elbow room, toe space, and knee space.

Reach is the distance you can comfortably reach for an object without having to lean over or stretch uncomfortably. For most adults, this is about 24 to 30 inches.

Elbow room is the side-to-side area you need in order to avoid feeling cramped. It becomes an important issue when two or more people must use the table at the same time.

Toe space is the horizontal distance a person needs under a table to feel comfortable when seated at the table.

Knee space is the vertical clearance a person needs under a table to feel comfortable when seated.

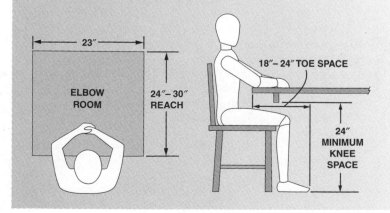

What style will it be?

There are dozens of styles to choose from when making a table, too many to show more than just a couple here. As designed, the writing table echoes a Country Empire style, popular in the first half of the nineteenth century. The top, with its distinctive corners, is sometimes called a *porringer top*. The rounded shapes at the corners reminded folks of the handle on a porringer, which in days gone by was a small bowl with a large handle.

To change the style, you need but change the profile of the top, legs, or aprons. In some cases, you may want to add rails or stretchers between the legs.

DESIGN SAVVY

In American furniture design, there is an important distinction between classic and country styles. Classic furniture was built for the trendy upper-class, and the design was often on the cutting edge of American decorative arts. A Classic Empire (or just plain *Empire*) table would typically display a good deal more craftsmanship than what you see here. That's because country furniture was built for the common folk. These were typically practical, inexpensive, simplified versions of the upper-class pieces. Often country cabinetmakers were just as skilled as classic craftsmen, but their clientele didn't have the wherewithal to pay for high style.

MISSION-STYLE WRITING TABLE

Toward the end of the nineteenth century, there was a reaction against the excessive ornamentation that had come to characterize high furniture styles and the watered-down interpretations that were being stamped out by furniture factories. The woodworkers who built Arts and Crafts (more commonly known as Mission) furniture revived medieval Gothic forms and advocated a return to more thoughtful craftsmanship. They still used modern techniques but paid careful attention to function, style, and structure. One of the most striking features of Mission furniture was the use of visible joinery as decoration. This is called *frank* joinery.

Crafted by Kevin P. Rodel and Susan Mack, Pownal, ME
Photo by Dennis Griggs

POSTMODERN-STYLE WRITING TABLE

The reaction against ornament that began in the late nineteenth century eventually resulted in austere looks such as the Modern and Contemporary styles. In these pieces, function was paramount. The form of the furniture, provided it was sufficiently graceful, was considered to be all the decoration necessary. In the 1970s, some craftsmen began to rebel against the dearth of ornamentation and began to mix decorative classic shapes and details back into their designs. This produced a contemporary form with a traditional touch. This writing table echoes the Queen Anne style, but it has many modern elements, such as the carved drawer pull.

Crafted by Richard Goehring, Gambier, OH

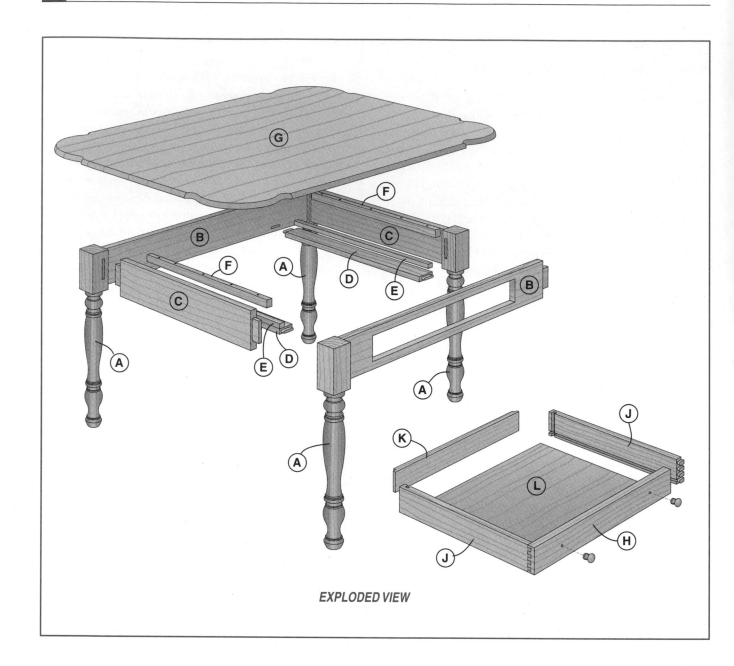

EXPLODED VIEW

WRITING TABLE ■ MATERIALS LIST *(Finished Dimensions)*

PARTS

A	Legs (4)	2¼″ × 2¼″ × 27″	**K**	Drawer back	½″ × 3¼″ × 20″
B	Front/back aprons (2)	¾″ × 5½″ × 30″	**L**	Drawer bottom*	¼″ × 19¼″ × 20″
C	Side aprons (2)	¾″ × 5½″ × 20″			
D	Drawer supports (2)	¾″ × 2″ × 19¾″			

Make this piece from plywood.

E	Drawer guides (2)	¾″ × ¾″ × 19″
F	Cleats (2)	¾″ × 1¼″ × 18¼″

HARDWARE

G	Top	¾″ × 29″ × 39″
H	Drawer front	¾″ × 3¾″ × 20½″
J	Drawer sides (2)	½″ × 3¾″ × 19⅜″

#10 × 1¾″ Roundhead wood screws (10)

#10 Flat washers (10)

1″ Drawer pulls (2)

How do I build it?

The first step in making a table is to *true* the parts — cut the stock for the legs and aprons straight and square.

PREPARING THE MATERIALS

To make the table as shown, you need approximately 21 board feet of 4/4 (four-quarters, or 1-inch-thick) lumber and 7 board feet of 10/4 (ten-quarters, or 2½-inch-thick) lumber. Bring the wood into your shop and let it dry for about a week so the boards won't be expanding or contracting after you cut them.

When the lumber is stable, study it and decide which boards you will use to make what parts. Then bust down the lumber into easily manageable sizes.

Plane the 4/4 stock to make the ¾-inch-thick and ½-inch-thick material that you need. True the leg stock, planing it to 2¼ inches square. Cut the parts to the sizes needed *except* for the top boards: Make these a little longer than specified. You need the extra length on the top boards to trim the glued-up stock to size.

GLUING UP THE TOP Lay out the boards you've selected for the top, and joint the edges. Normally, I make wide table tops with the heart of the tree facing up — that is, all the annual rings in the board cup *up*. Since the heartwood in most wood species has more color, the top looks better with the boards arranged this way. More important, since lumber tends to cup opposite the annual rings, the top will want to rise in the center. The screws and the cleats can prevent this easily. But if the top were to cup in the opposite direction, it might curl up at the edges.

SHOP SAVVY

To true leg stock, joint one surface (1), then joint an adjacent surface square to the first (2). Mark the two surfaces you have jointed so you remember which they are. Plane the two remaining surfaces parallel to the jointed surfaces; plane both without changing the thickness adjustment (3, 4). The resulting stock will be perfectly straight and square.

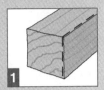 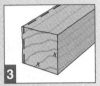 

NO PROBLEM ■ *Jointing with a Router*

You're new to woodworking and don't yet have a jointer. Or your jointer's down because the knives are at the sharpening service. No problem. A table-mounted router, properly set up, makes a world-class edge jointer.

Using double-faced carpet tape, stick a scrap of plastic laminate to the outfeed face of your fence. This will advance the outfeed surface a tiny fraction of an inch in front of the infeed surface — like the two surfaces of a jointer. Mount a straight bit in the router and adjust the fence position so the bit just shaves the edge of a board as you guide it along the fence. The stock removed must be equal to the laminate thickness.

To check your setup, select a 2-foot-long scrap and joint 2 to 3 inches along one edge, at the leading end, creating a "snipe." Shade the surface of the snipe with a pencil. Turn the board end for end and joint the entire edge, cutting the snipe last. If the fence is positioned correctly, the router bit will just kiss the pencil marks, making them appear lighter but not removing them completely.

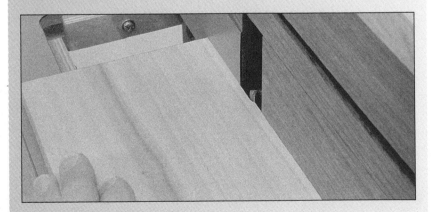

ANOTHER WAY TO GO

When gluing up boards to make wide stock, it's usually sufficient just to joint the edges. Occasionally, however, I've had to cut a glue joint at the edges. A glue joint is a zigzag cut that creates interlocking tongues and grooves at the edges. This increases the glue surface and the joint strength somewhat. But the real value is that it automatically aligns the boards when you assemble them. If you're gluing up a lot of narrow strips or the boards are slightly twisted, this can keep you from losing your religion in frustration.

Cut the glue joints with a special bit on a table-mounted router. Unlike a tongue-and-groove joint, you don't need two bits to make this edge joint. A single bit with one setup creates the interlocking edges.

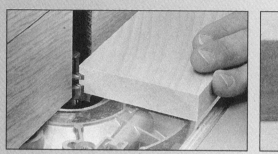

GLUING UP THE FRONT APRON In the Materials List, the front apron is listed as one board and the drawer front is listed as another. You can do it that way if you want to paint the aprons, as I have done — no one will see the differing wood grain. But if you plan to apply a clear finish, you may want to make the parts from the same board so the wood grain appears continuous. To do this, cut the stock for the front apron about ½ inch longer and wider than needed. Joint the top edge, and rip a ¾-inch-wide strip from it. Then rip a 3¾-inch-wide strip and cut that into three parts, as shown. Set aside the middle part — this will become the drawer front. Glue the remaining parts back together in their original position and trim the apron to size.

> **Look Here!** For more information on gluing up a front with a drawer opening, see "Preparing the Materials" on page 9.

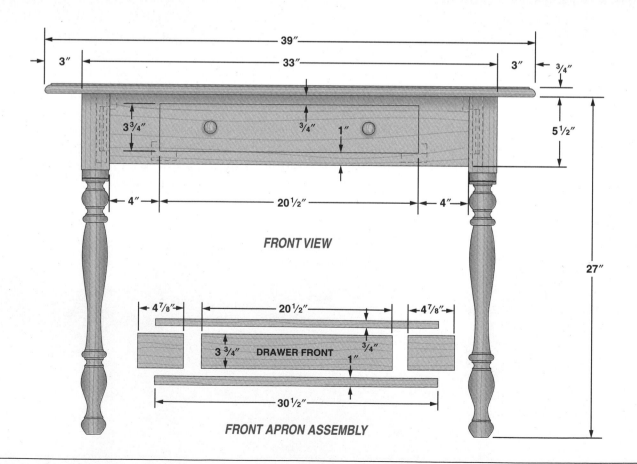

FRONT VIEW

FRONT APRON ASSEMBLY

JOINING LEGS AND APRONS

The traditional joinery for leg-and-apron constructions is the mortise-and-tenon joint. Table legs are prone to *racking*. They are pulled sideways like a lever every time you lean on the table or scoot it across the floor. This puts tremendous stresses on the joints between the legs and aprons. Of all the possible joints you can use, most craftsmen consider the mortise-and-tenon best at withstanding this racking stress.

MAKING MORTISE-AND-TENON JOINTS To rout a mortise-and-tenon joint, you must first cut a mortise in the leg, then create a protruding tenon on the adjoining apron to fit it. There is nothing complex about this process; you are, in fact, making two simple joints. The mortise is just a stopped groove, closed at both ends. The tenon is created by routing one or more rabbets in the end of a board. Each rabbet forms a cheek and a shoulder.

Here are a few tips for routing mortise-and-tenon joints:

■ When laying out the joints, score the shoulders of the tenon with a bench knife or a marking knife.

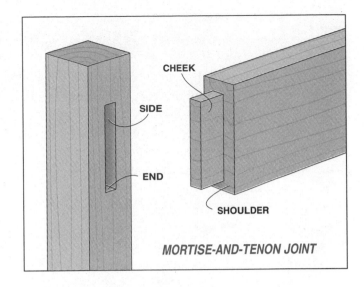

MORTISE-AND-TENON JOINT

This will prevent the wood fibers from chipping or tearing when you cut the tenon shoulders.

■ Make the mortise first, then fit the tenon to it. It's easier to trim a tenon with a plane or a chisel than it is to enlarge a mortise.

■ Try for a *slip fit*. There should be no discernible slop, but you should be able to put the joint together and take it apart without using a mallet.

(continued on page 41)

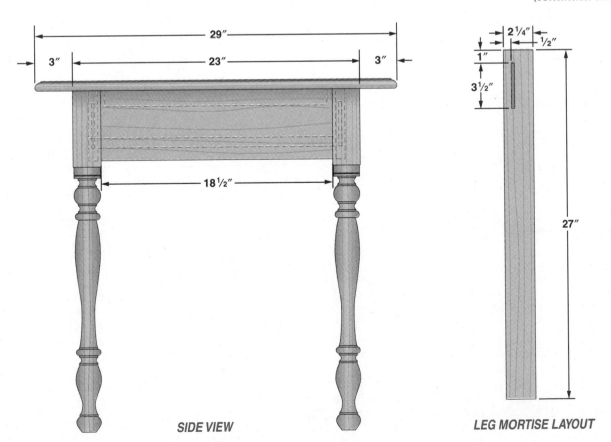

SIDE VIEW

LEG MORTISE LAYOUT

METHODS OF WORK ■ *Routing Mortises and Tenons*

Rout mortises with *straight* or *mortising* bits. For deep mortises, consider an *upcut spiral* bit. The flutes on these bits clear the wood chips from the mortise as they cut, in the same manner that a twist-drill bit does.

There are many techniques for routing mortises. These are the two that Jim and I use most often.

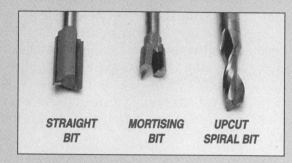

STRAIGHT BIT **MORTISING BIT** **UPCUT SPIRAL BIT**

ROUTING MORTISES ON A ROUTER TABLE

1 When you have just a few mortises to make, it's usually easiest to create them on a router table. However, you must do some creative layout work to compensate for the fact that you can't see the cut as it progresses. When marking the mortise, transfer the lines that indicate the ends of the mortise to the surface that will face out (or away from the fence) as you cut.

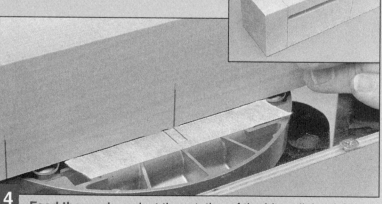

2 Additionally, stick a piece of masking tape to the table top in front of the bit. Using the head of a combination square, make two marks that indicate the diameter of the bit on the tape.

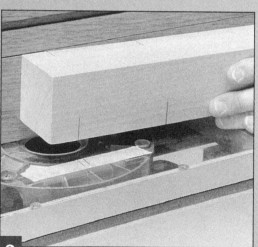

3 Adjust the depth of cut so the bit will cut no more than ⅛ inch deep on the first pass. Hold the stock over the bit, keeping it pressed against the fence. Then slowly lower it down onto the bit.

4 Feed the work against the rotation of the bit until the right-hand mark on the stock aligns with the right-hand mark on the tape. Then feed it in the opposite direction until the left-hand marks align. Then raise the bit another ⅛ inch, and repeat until you have routed the mortise to the depth you want. **Warning: Because you're *back-routing* (cutting with the rotation of the bit rather than against it) during this part of the operation, you must be especially careful. Keep a firm grip on the stock, and feed very slowly. This is why I suggest shallow cuts.**

ROUTING MORTISES WITH A HAND-HELD ROUTER AND TEMPLATE

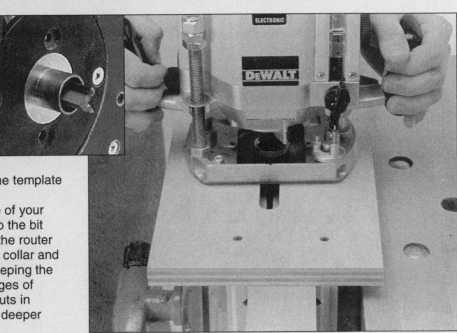

If you have a large number of mortises to make, the job will go faster if you make a *routing template.* The template guides the router and halts the cut at the same points every time. You save time because you don't have to lay out each mortise. Just align the template on the stock, and clamp it in place.

Mount a guide collar on the base of your router and adjust the depth of cut so the bit protrudes through the collar. Place the router on the template, inserting the guide collar and bit in the cutout. Cut the mortise, keeping the guide collar pressed against the edges of the cutout. As always, make deep cuts in several passes, routing just 1/8 inch deeper with each pass.

QUICK FIXTURE ■ *Mortising Template*

To make a mortising template, cut an opening in a piece of plywood or hard-board to guide a router outfitted with a guide collar. The opening must be slightly longer and wider than the mortise to compensate for the difference in diameters between the bit and the guide collar. How much longer and wider? Subtract the bit diameter (BD) from the collar diameter (CD) and add the result to the length (L) and to the width (W) of the mortise you wish to rout. This will give you the length and width of the opening in the template (TL and TW).

$$(CD - BD) + L = TL$$
$$(CD - BD) + W = TW$$

Attach cleats to the template to help position it and secure it to the work.

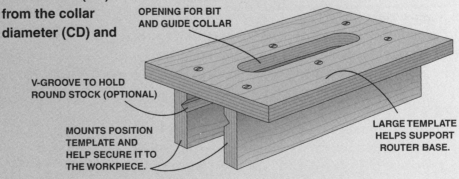

If you wish to rout mortises in round stock, cut V-grooves in the cleats to straddle the work.

OPENING FOR BIT AND GUIDE COLLAR

V-GROOVE TO HOLD ROUND STOCK (OPTIONAL)

MOUNTS POSITION TEMPLATE AND HELP SECURE IT TO THE WORKPIECE.

LARGE TEMPLATE HELPS SUPPORT ROUTER BASE.

(continued)

METHODS OF WORK ■ *Routing Mortises and Tenons* — CONTINUED

1 **To rout a tenon on a router table,** use a simple *tenoning jig* as a carriage or a pusher to feed the work over the bit. Position the fence so the distance from the face to the *farthest* side of the router bit is equal to the length of the tenon. Adjust the depth of cut, and clamp the stock to the tenoning jig. Slowly feed the work over the bit, guiding the jig along the fence. This will create a single cheek and shoulder.

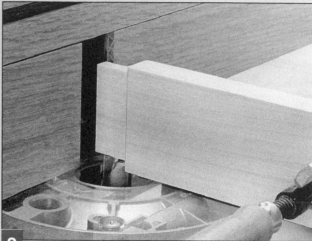

2 **Turn the stock** and repeat this procedure, cutting the edges and faces as needed to create the tenon. If the tenon is longer than the bit is wide, cut it in several passes, making it longer with each pass. **Note:** The router leaves round corners in the mortise, yet the completed tenon is square. To fit the tenon to the mortise, either square the corners of the mortise with a chisel or round the corners of the tenon with a rasp.

QUICK FIXTURE ■ *Router Table Tenoning Jig*

Most straight bits are "top-cutting." That is, both the sides *and* the top or end of the bit will cut wood. Because of this, you don't have to stand a board up on end to cut a tenon on a router table, as you do on a table saw. A router table "tenoning jig" is really just a pusher with long guiding surfaces.

Make the base from a scrap of plywood and the face from hardwood. Cut a notch in the inside edge of the base — this accommodates the clamps or gives you a good handhold to help secure the work.

The face also serves as a backup to prevent tear-out when you rout. When the face becomes chewed up, adhere another board to it with double-faced carpet tape to create a "secondary" face.

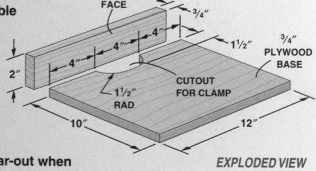

FACE

3/4"

4"

4"

4"

4"

2"

1 1/2"

3/4"
PLYWOOD
BASE

1 1/2"
RAD

CUTOUT
FOR CLAMP

10"

12"

EXPLODED VIEW

After routing the joints, square the round corners of the mortises with a chisel to fit the tenons, or round the square corners of the tenons with a rasp to fit the mortises, whichever you prefer.

Also miter the ends of the tenons, as shown in the *Apron-to-Leg Joinery Detail*. This isn't always necessary in leg-and-apron assemblies, but it is in this one. If the tenons aren't mitered, they will interfere with one another.

JOINING THE DRAWER SUPPORTS TO THE APRONS

The drawer supports are mortised into the inside surfaces of the front and back aprons. Rout mortises in the aprons and then rout the tenons on the ends of the supports.

TURNING THE TABLE LEGS

Once you've fitted the mortises and tenons, turn the table legs. These are fairly complex shapes, and if you're an "occasional turner" like me, you may be worried about getting all four of them the same. *Don't be.* There are some simple secrets for duplicating legs.

OOPS!

Cut a tenon so it's too loose in the mortise? No problem. Glue wood-veneer shims to the cheeks and let dry. Then, if the tenon is too tight, shave the veneer with a router plane.

DUPLICATING TURNED LEGS (WITHOUT A DUPLICATOR) The most important of these secrets is to turn the shaped parts of each leg *to the same diameters*. When you study the *Leg Layout*, note that these are divided up into *major diameters* (on the left side of the layout) and *minor diameters* (on the right side). The major diameters include the crest of beads, flats, and the widest portion of tapers. Minor diameters include the bottoms of coves and the narrowest portions of tapers.

Make a template that includes these diameters, then use it to locate the diameters on each leg. Use calipers to measure the diameters as you turn. Make sure they're the same from leg to leg. And that's all you have to do! The turned legs will be remarkably similar.

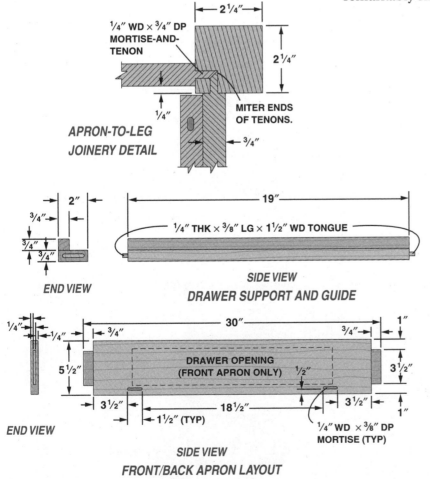

APRON-TO-LEG JOINERY DETAIL

DRAWER SUPPORT AND GUIDE

FRONT/BACK APRON LAYOUT

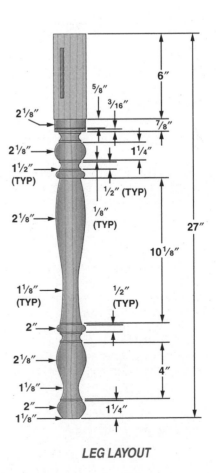

LEG LAYOUT

METHODS OF WORK ■ *Duplicating Turned Legs*

1 Draw a full-sized plan of the leg. Using spray adhesive, attach it to a thin piece of plywood or hardboard. With a scroll saw, saber saw, or coping saw, cut out a negative of the profile, making a *reverse template*. Mark the major and minor diameters on the template.

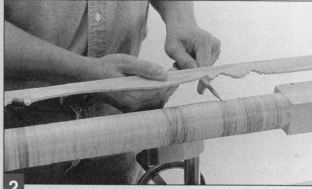

2 Round the stock, then use the template to mark the locations of the major and minor diameters. **Tip: When turning a complex profile, shade beads a light color and the coves darker. This will help eliminate confusion when turning the profile.**

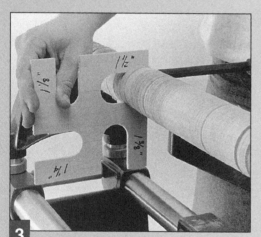

3 Turn the major and minor diameters with a parting tool, using calipers to make sure each diameter is reasonably precise.

QUICK FIXTURE ■ *Fixed Calipers*

To save time when measuring diameters, make a set of *fixed* calipers. Cut the openings to correspond to the diameters in the turning. Just inside each opening, make a 1/16-inch step to serve as an "early warning" device. When the calipers slip over the turning up to the step, you know you're getting close to the desired diameter.

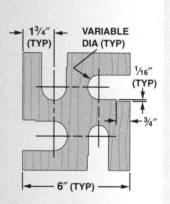

FIXED CALIPERS LAYOUT

4 Turn the beads, coves, and flats, stopping when you reach the diameters you turned with the parting tool. After careful marking and turning of the shapes, the spindles will turn out remarkably similar to one another. To further ensure that the profiles are alike, compare the legs to the template as the profile evolves.

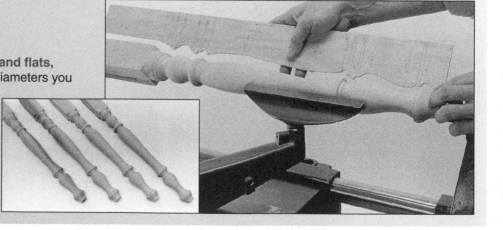

MAKING THE TABLE TOP

The table top is designed to be user-friendly. The porringer shape eliminates the sharp corners, so you're less likely to experience a painful bump. The thumbnail shape at the edge makes it more comfortable when you're writing or typing — there are no sharp arrises to dig into your wrists or forearms.

CUTTING THE PORRINGER PROFILE Lay out the corners of the top as shown in the *Top View*. Cut the shapes with a saber saw or band saw, then sand the cut edges smooth. Take care that the finished curves are *fair*, with no flat spots or sharp changes in the contour.

ROUTING THE THUMBNAIL EDGE The thumbnail shape is a compound profile, made up of simpler shapes. Because of this, you must cut the profile in two steps. Make the small bead first, then the larger bead and the step.

Rout a thumbnail edge in two passes. First rout the smaller bead around the perimeter of the bottom surface, using a quarter-round (or roundover) bit *(top)*. Then make the large bead and step on the top surface. By routing the smaller bead first, you leave more stock at the edge to guide the router during the second pass *(bottom)*.

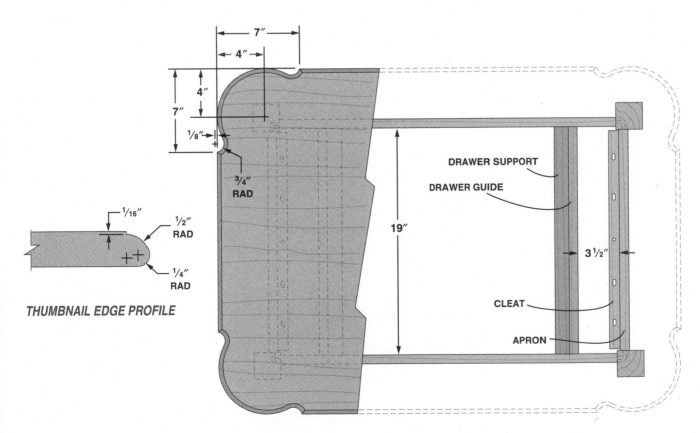

THUMBNAIL EDGE PROFILE

7″
4″
4″
7″
1/8″
3/4″ RAD
1/16″
1/2″ RAD
1/4″ RAD

DRAWER SUPPORT
DRAWER GUIDE
19″
3 1/2″
CLEAT
APRON

TOP VIEW

MAKING AND FITTING THE DRAWER

The front corners on this drawer are joined by *half-blind* dovetails, so called because you can't see the joints from one direction. The dovetails are hidden when you're looking at the drawer front.

ROUTING HALF-BLIND DOVETAILS You can rout these dovetails using a commercial template. So why would I recommend a store-bought tool for half-blind dovetails when I went through all the trouble to show you how to make your own jig for through dovetails in the last project? Good question. I recommend a shop-made jig when (1) it will do a job for which there is no commercial tool, (2) it will do a job better than a commercial tool, or (3) it will save you money *and* time. Through dovetail jigs are absurdly expensive; it pays to make your own. Half-blind dovetail jigs, on the other hand, are plentiful and cheap.

And it would be difficult to make something that saves you more time. Half-blind dovetail jigs allow you to cut the pins and the tails *in a single step.* Mount both adjoining boards in the fixture, and mount a dovetail bit and a guide collar on the router. Then simply follow the comb with the guide collar. The dovetail bit will cut through the tail board, routing tails. Then it will continue a short distance into the pin board, making pins.

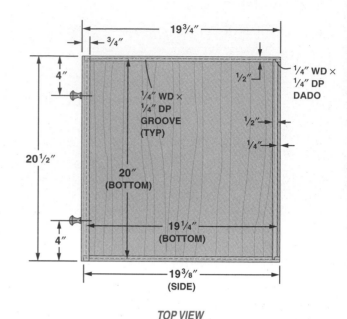

TOP VIEW

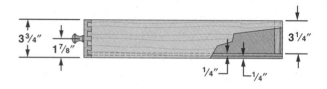

SIDE VIEW
DRAWER

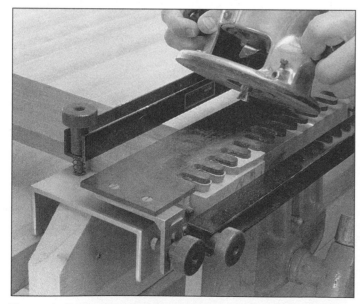

To rout half-blind dovetails, secure both boards in the jig. The tail board is held vertically, its end flush with the top face of the horizontal pin board. The inside surfaces of both boards should be visible. Cut both boards in a single pass.

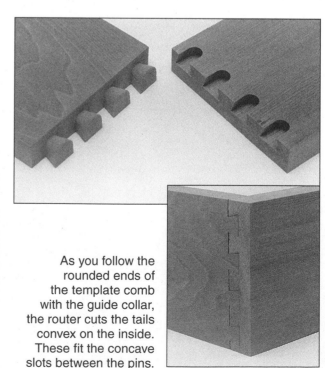

As you follow the rounded ends of the template comb with the guide collar, the router cuts the tails convex on the inside. These fit the concave slots between the pins.

It's *almost* foolproof. There are, however, some tricks to remember. The distance between the tails is fixed. If you want the joints to have a traditional look with split pins top and bottom, you must adjust the height of the drawer to the jig. Also, carefully mark the inside surfaces of the drawer parts before routing them. The insides must face up and out as you work.

REMAINING JOINERY The remaining joinery we ran into in the preceding chapter. The back corners are joined by rabbet-and-dado joints, while the bottom floats in grooves.

> **Look Here!** For more information on routing rabbets, dadoes, and grooves, see page 14.

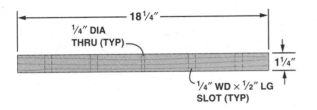

18¼″

¼″ DIA THRU (TYP)

1¼″

¼″ WD × ½″ LG SLOT (TYP)

CLEAT LAYOUT

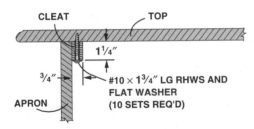

CLEAT   TOP

1¼″

¾″   #10 × 1¾″ LG RHWS AND FLAT WASHER (10 SETS REQ'D)

APRON

TOP-TO-APRON JOINERY DETAIL

CONSIDER THIS
Ever wonder why the front corners of a drawer are treated differently than the back ones are? It's because the pulls are mounted on the front, so these corners must withstand more stress.

ASSEMBLING THE TABLE

Once you have cut the joinery, finish sand the parts and assemble them. Start by joining the legs to the front and back aprons. While the glue is drying on these two assemblies, glue the drawer guides to the drawer supports. Then add the side aprons and support assemblies.

ATTACHING THE TABLE TOP The top must float so it can expand independently of the leg-and-apron assembly. To allow for this movement, Jim and I routed slots in two cleats, and glued the cleats to the side aprons. To secure the top, we drove round-head screws through the slots and into the bottom surface of the table. Incidentally, our table top had cupped by the time we got around to doing this. The screws and cleats pulled it flat again.

FINISHING THE TABLE

Empire pieces were often painted — sometimes partially painted. I elected to paint the leg-and-apron assembly but apply a clear finish to the top. Much of the reason for this decision was that the lower part of the table was made from scraps of several different woods, while the top was cut from a beautiful piece of curly white oak.

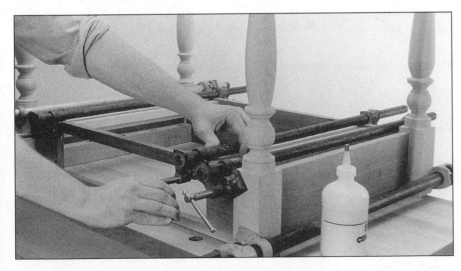

When assembling the table, rest it upside down on a flat surface. After you clamp up the legs and aprons, turn it right side up and make sure all four feet are touching the surface to ensure that the table won't rock when used.

ANOTHER WAY TO GO ■ *Routing Round and Oval Table Tops*

As designed, the top of the writing table is roughly rectangular — an easy shape to create with a table saw. But what if you wanted to make a circular or an elliptical table top? The best tool for these jobs is the router. With the aid of a *trammel jig,* you can rout circles and ovals more precisely than you can by laying them out and cutting them with any other tool. Furthermore, you can use a trammel jig to "scoop" a round or oval table top, creating raised "piecrust" edges.

ROUTING ROUND TABLE TOPS

To rout a circle, swing the router around a pivot as if it were a giant beam compass. However, sometimes you don't want to mar your work by drilling a hole or driving a screw to make a pivot. The trammel jig includes a separate *pivot block* that you can easily attach to a smooth surface.

1　**Mark the center** of the circle you want to rout with a large "X." Secure the pivot block to the work with double-faced carpet tape, aligning the corners of the block with the arms of the "X."

2　**Mount a straight bit** in your router, and attach the router to the end of the beam on the trammel jig. Drive a roundhead screw through the beam and into the pivot block. The distance from the screw to the edge of the bit should be equal to the radius of the circle you want to make. **Tip: As designed, the beam has pivot holes every ½ inch. You can adjust the radius of the circle by varying the diameter of the bit or drilling new holes in the beam.**

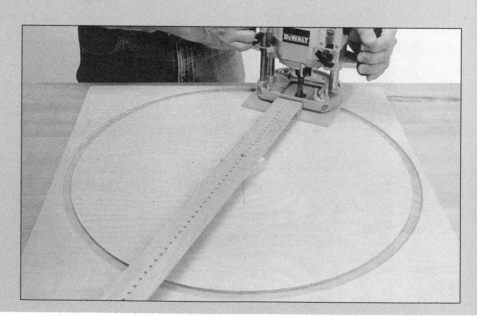

3　**Swing the router** and the beam around the pivot screw, cutting a circle. If necessary, make several passes, cutting no more than ⅛ inch deep with each pass. When the circle is complete, remove the pivot block and discard the tape.

ROUTING OVAL TABLE TOPS

To rout an oval shape, you must swing the router around two movable pivots, forming a "double trammel." The pivots slide back and forth in two dovetail slots at right angles to one another. One pivot controls the length of the oval, or its *major axis*, and the other the width, or *minor axis*. See the plans for a double trammel jig on page 49.

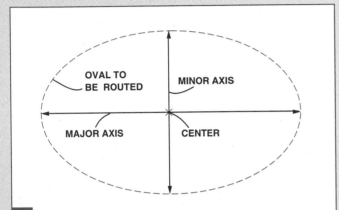

1 Lay out the major and minor axes of the oval that you want to rout. Draw two lines that cross at right angles to one another, then measure the length of the oval on one line and the width on the other. The lines must intersect at the center of the oval, halfway along the length of each axis.

2 Attach the double trammel pivot block to the workpiece with double-faced carpet tape, aligning the center of the dovetail slots with the axes of the oval. Attach the router to the beam, and align the beam with the major axis. Center the minor pivot (the pivot that moves along the minor axis) over the center of the oval. Position the router so the *inside* cutting edge of the bit (the edge nearest the center) is even with one end of the major axis, then fasten the beam to the pivot.

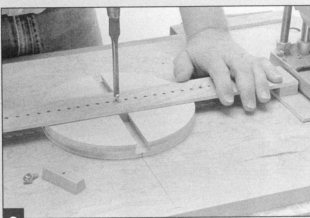

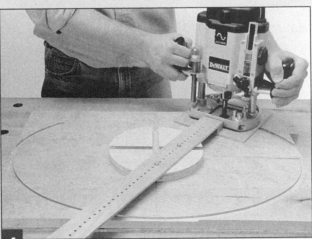

3 Swing the beam 90 degrees, aligning it with the minor axis. Position the major pivot over the center of the oval. Position the router so the bit is even with one end of the minor axis, and fasten the beam to the pivot. The beam should now be fastened to *both* pivots. To check the setup, swing the router once around the pivot block with the power off. The bit should pass over the ends of the major and minor axes.

4 Turn on the router, adjust the depth of cut for a shallow bite, and swing the router around the pivots. As you rout, pull *gently* outward. The slight tension will take any play out of the mechanical system, helping to create a smooth, precise oval. Make several passes, routing just a little deeper with each pass.

(continued)

ANOTHER WAY TO GO ■ *Routing Round and Oval Table Tops* — CONTINUED

SCOOPING A PIECRUST TOP

To make a "piecrust" table top, you must scoop out the interior surface, creating a raised lip around the circumference of the top. To do this you'll need *two* routing jigs — the Router Trammel Jig (page 49) and the extended base that was used on the Router Planing Jig (page 10).

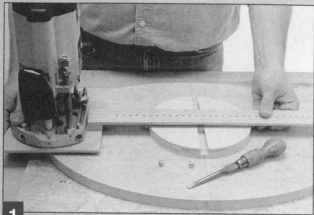

1   First, rout the table top and decide how wide the lip will be (as viewed from above). To the width, add half the diameter of the router bit you used to cut the circle or oval and half the diameter of the bit you will use to cut the inside circumference of the lip. This is how far you must move the beam on the pivot or pivots, bringing the router closer to the center of the table top. For example, consider you want to create a ³/₈-inch-wide lip on an oval table top. You routed the top with a ³/₄-inch straight bit and will cut the inside surface of the lip with a ¹/₂-inch 3-in-1 bit. You must move the beam on *both* trammel pivots 1 inch: $3/8 + (3/4 \div 2) + (1/2 \div 2) = 1$.

2   Rout the inside circumference of the lip with a 3-in-1 bit. This bit cuts a recess with rounded corners between the bottom and the sides. (A straight bit cuts square corners, and the transition from the bottom to the side may appear too abrupt.) To create a lip with shaped sides, use a *point-cut bit*. These are available in cove, bead, and ogee shapes.

CORE-BOX (COVE) BIT   POINT-CUT OGEE BIT

3   Using the same 3-in-1 bit and an extended base to support the router, thin out the top inside the groove you just cut. Start removing stock near the lip around the outside edge of the table top, and slowly work your way toward the center.

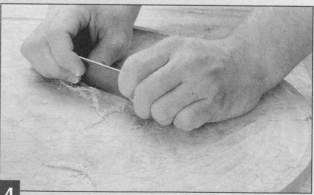

4   Carefully sand or scrape the thinned-out area to blend the inside of the lip with the top surface and to smooth the small ridges and steps left by the router. If you've routed a shaped lip, be careful not to sand so much that you distort the profile or make its features indistinct.

QUICK FIXTURE ■ *Router Trammel Jig*

This trammel jig enables you to rout both circles and ovals of different sizes. The router attaches to a beam, and the beam can be fastened to two different pivots. Attach it to the simple block with a single pivot to make circles. For ovals, fasten it to the grooved block with two sliding pivots.

As shown, the beam is 32 inches long and has pivot holes regularly spaced every ½ inch. This lets you rout circles over 60 inches in diameter and ovals up to 48 inches along the major axis. For larger workpieces, make a longer beam. Attach the router to the end of the beam with a mounting plate made of thin plywood. I've always removed the sole of the router and screwed it to mounting plates such as these, but Jim has found that it's just as secure — and a whole lot less trouble — to stick the router to the plate with double-faced carpet tape.

The circle pivot is just a square block with a pilot hole in the center of one face. The oval pivot has two dovetail slots that cross at right angles

in the middle of the block. To cut these slots, first rout ordinary grooves with a straight bit to remove most of the stock, then create the dovetail shape with a dovetail bit. Cut the sliding pivot blocks to fit the slots as closely as possible.

The size of the oval pivot block depends on the size of the oval you want to rout. Subtract the minor axis from the major axis — the result is the minimum length and width of the pivot block. Add 1 more inch so the sliding pivots won't accidentally slip out of their slots.

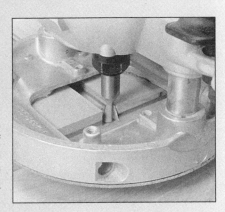

To make a dovetail slot, rout a rectangular groove to remove most of the waste, then enlarge the groove with a dovetail bit.

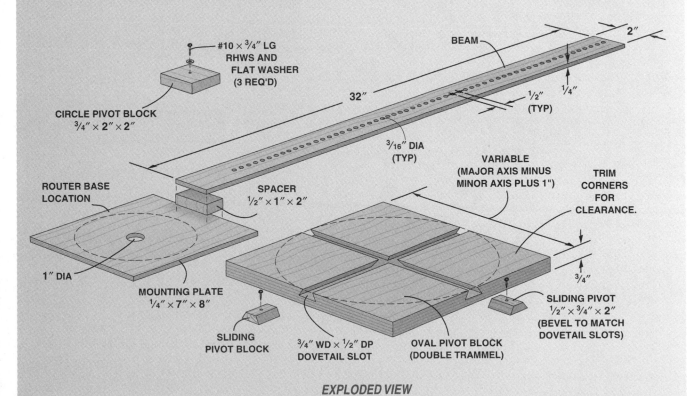

#10 × ¾″ LG RHWS AND FLAT WASHER (3 REQ'D)

CIRCLE PIVOT BLOCK
¾″ × 2″ × 2″

ROUTER BASE LOCATION

1″ DIA

MOUNTING PLATE
¼″ × 7″ × 8″

SPACER
½″ × 1″ × 2″

SLIDING PIVOT BLOCK

¾″ WD × ½″ DP DOVETAIL SLOT

OVAL PIVOT BLOCK
(DOUBLE TRAMMEL)

BEAM

2″

32″

¼″

½″
(TYP)

³⁄₁₆″ DIA
(TYP)

VARIABLE
(MAJOR AXIS MINUS
MINOR AXIS PLUS 1″)

TRIM CORNERS FOR CLEARANCE.

¾″

SLIDING PIVOT
½″ × ¾″ × 2″
(BEVEL TO MATCH DOVETAIL SLOTS)

EXPLODED VIEW

ALMOST A
Grandfather Clock

In this chapter...

PRACTICAL KNOW-HOW

Making Bracket Feet	63
Routing Molded Shapes	67
Routing Spline Grooves	69
Making Gooseneck Molding	72

JIGS AND FIXTURES

Long Pusher	68
Featherboard	68

SHOP SOLUTIONS

Quartering a Turning	64
Joining a Molded Door Frame	65

Routers were originally invented to cut profiles and molded shapes. In fact, during the early years of the twentieth century, they were sold as "hand shapers." This is still one of the most useful and unique features of a router.

And there are few projects where you use a router for shaping as much as you do in a grandfather clock. At first glance, a classic clock case looks as if it were made of moldings — there are shapes stacked on shapes from the bottom of the clock to its very top. This clock, made by Jim McCann, is no exception. A few of these shapes — the columns on the base and the hood — are turned on a lathe, but all the others are created with a router and common shaping bits — roundover, bead, cove, and ogee.

What size should it be?

When you start out to build a clock, you are actually building the clock *case,* a wooden cabinet designed to hold the clockwork and protect it from dust. The size of the case depends not only on the works but also on what kind of clock case you want to make.

TYPES OF CASE CLOCKS There are four common types of clock cases.

■ The *grandfather clock* is the largest of case clocks, typically standing over 82 inches high, according to most antique clock specialists. Jim calls his piece "almost a grandfather clock" because it lacks less than ½ inch in height to qualify as a true, undisputed grandfather clock. The term, by the way, dates from 1878 when Henry Clay Works wrote a popular song, "My Grandfather's Clock." Before then, these were commonly referred to as *tall case clocks.*

■ A *grandmother clock,* or *dwarf tall case clock,* stands on the floor or a low table, but it is about two-thirds the size of a proper grandfather clock. Most are between 45 and 60 inches tall.

■ A *shelf clock* is meant to rest on a shelf or mantel and is usually between 24 and 40 inches tall.

■ A *wall clock* hangs on the wall and can be almost any size. Most are between 24 and 60 inches tall.

A *grandfather clock* is commonly 82 inches tall or taller; *grandmother clocks (shown)* are about two-thirds that size.

A *shelf clock* is typically between 24 and 40 inches tall.

A *wall clock* can be as large as a grandmother clock or as small as a shelf clock. The major difference is that the case is designed to hang on a wall rather than rest on a shelf or floor.

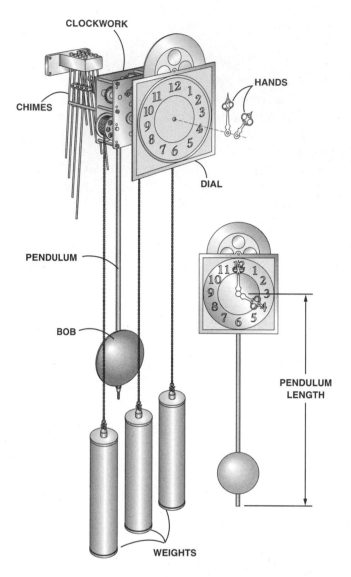

CLOCKWORK

CHIMES

HANDS

DIAL

PENDULUM

BOB

PENDULUM LENGTH

WEIGHTS

A clockwork consists of several pieces of hardware, all of which must fit inside the clock case. The *works* themselves — the gears and gizmos that keep the time and make the hands go around — are assembled in a compact package with one or more protruding brackets so you can mount them to the clock board. If the works sound the hours, they will include several *chimes* — metal rods that ring when struck by tiny hammers in the works. These, too, are mounted on a bracket so they can be attached to the clock board. A clock face or *dial* attaches to the front of the works. A post protrudes through the dial, and the clock *hands* are mounted on it. The *pendulum* and *bob* hang from the works. The length of the pendulum is measured from the center of the dial to the end of the pendulum bar. Finally, some clocks are driven by *weights.* These also hang from the bottom of the works.

Tip: Of all the dimensions associated with the clockwork, the most commonly overlooked is the length of the post on which the hands are mounted. I've seen several clocks where the glass on the hood door bangs into the tip of the post.

FITTING THE CASE AROUND THE WORKS No matter what kind of clock case you decide to make, it should perform three important functions.

■ It should completely surround the clockwork to protect it from dust and dirt.

■ It must display the clock face prominently at a level where it can be easily read.

■ It should enclose the pendulum to keep it from being bumped, but not interfere with the *swing* of the pendulum.

Additionally, if the clockwork sounds the hours, the case must have soundholes so as not to muffle the chimes.

DESIGN SAVVY

On a grandfather or large grandmother clock, the clockwork is typically attached to the back of the case, or the clockboard. To provide easy access to the clockwork for cleaning and repairs, design the hood so it slips off the front, exposing the works.

On a shelf clock, wall clock, and small grandmother clock, the works are typically attached to a board that also holds the clock face or dial. By making the top removable and letting the face board "float" in grooves, you can slide the works out of the clock for cleaning and repairs.

What style will it be?

Jim built his clock in a classic eighteenth-century Queen Anne style. The bracket feet on the base, the gooseneck moldings on the hood, the profiles of the moldings all make use of the traditional S-curve or *ogee*. The ogee became a popular design element in the Queen Anne period (1725 to 1750) and has remained so ever since.

However, there are many other ways to build a clock case, many of them simpler and less ornate. Here are two possibilities:

SHAKER STYLE

The Shakers are a strict religious order founded in 1790 on the principles of equality, celibacy, communal living away from the outside world, and asceticism. As the sect grew, they began to make their own furniture. However, because the Shakers believed that "beauty rests on utility," they stripped their designs of almost all ornament. The tall case clock shown here is well designed and well crafted, but the case is simple and functional.

Courtesy Barbara and Glen Wuest, Milwaukee, WI.

MISSION STYLE

A century after the Shakers were founded, some furniture designers began to rebel against the excessive ornament of the Victorian period and the rise of mass-produced furniture. The furniture makers of the Arts and Crafts (or Mission) style believed in a return to "honest" craftsmanship and simpler styles. They revived old Gothic forms from almost 400 years ago and used them to create a distinct style, as this tall case clock shows.

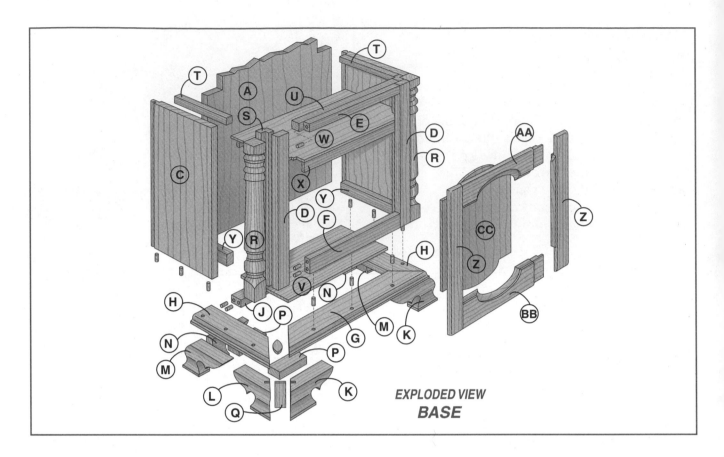

EXPLODED VIEW
BASE

GRANDFATHER CLOCK ■ *MATERIALS LIST* (Finished Dimensions)

PARTS — BASE

A	Clock board*	¾″ × 16⅝″ × 71⅝″
B	Clock shelf* *(shown on page 56)*	¾″ × 5⅛″ × 12½″
C	Base sides (2)	¾″ × 8⅜″ × 17½″
D	Front frame stiles (2)	¾″ × 1″ × 17½″
E	Front frame top rail	¾″ × 1″ × 12¾″
F	Front frame bottom rail	¾″ × 2¼″ × 12¾″
G	Base frame front	¾″ × 2¾″ × 18¼″
H	Base frame sides (2)	¾″ × 2¾″ × 10⅛″
J	Base frame back	¾″ × 1⅜″ × 12¾″
K	Front feet (2)	1¾″ × 3″ × 6″
L	Front side feet (2)	1¾″ × 3″ × 5½″
M	Back side feet (2)	1¾″ × 3″ × 4½″
N	Back feet (2)	¾″ × 3″ × 6″
P	Glue blocks (4)	¾″ × 2¼″ × 3″
Q	Splines (2)	¼″ × 3″ × 1″
R	Quarter base columns (2)	1¼″ × 1¼″ × 17½″
S	Corner blocks (2)	1″ × 1″ × 17½″
T	Side cleats (2)	¾″ × ¾″ × 7⅛″

U	Front cleat	¾″ × ¾″ × 13¾″
V	Bottom*	¼″ × 6″ × 12¾″
W	False bottom*	¼″ × 8⅛″ × 15¾″
X	Front/back false bottom supports (2)	½″ × 1¼″ × 15¾″
Y	Side false bottom supports (2)	½″ × 1¼″ × 7⅛″
Z	Base door stiles (2)	¾″ × 1¾″ × 15¾″
AA	Base door top rail	¾″ × 3⅛″ × 13½″
BB	Base door bottom rail	¾″ × 3½″ × 13½″
CC	Base door panel	¼″ × 10¼″ × 14½″

Make these parts from plywood.

HARDWARE

#0 Biscuits (2)

¼″ dia. × 1″ dowels (19)

Offset hinges and mounting screws (2)

#8 × 1¼″ Flathead wood screws (24–28)

#6 × ½″ Flathead wood screws (4)

Door pull and catch

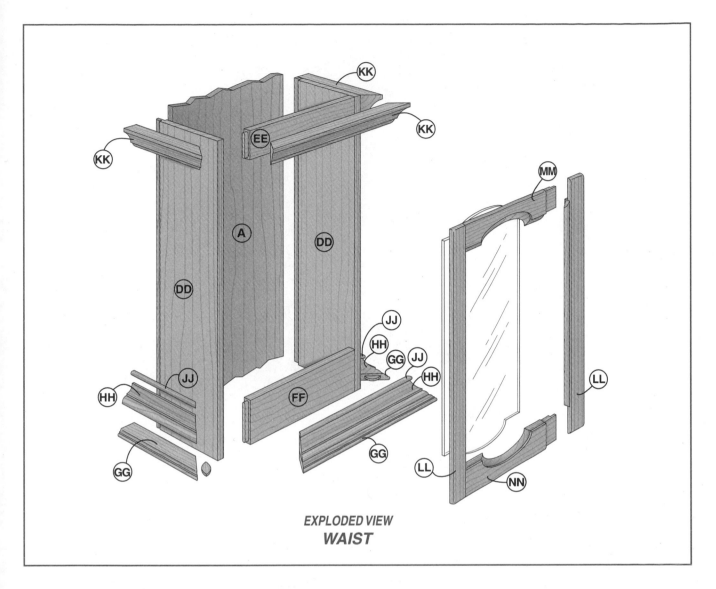

EXPLODED VIEW
WAIST

GRANDFATHER CLOCK ■ MATERIALS LIST *(Finished Dimensions)* — *CONTINUED*

PARTS — WAIST

DD	Waist sides (2)	$\frac{3}{4}'' \times 8\frac{1}{8}'' \times 37\frac{1}{4}''$
EE	Waist top rail	$\frac{3}{4}'' \times 3\frac{1}{2}'' \times 13\frac{3}{4}''$
FF	Waist bottom rail	$\frac{3}{4}'' \times 5\frac{1}{2}'' \times 13\frac{3}{4}''$
GG	Bottom lower waist molding (total)	$\frac{3}{4}'' \times 2\frac{1}{16}'' \times 48''$
HH	Center lower waist molding (total)	$1\frac{1}{2}'' \times 2\frac{1}{8}'' \times 44''$
JJ	Top lower waist molding (total)	$\frac{7}{16}'' \times \frac{1}{2}'' \times 44''$
KK	Upper waist molding (total)	$1\frac{1}{2}'' \times 2\frac{1}{2}'' \times 44''$
LL	Waist door stiles (2)	$\frac{3}{4}'' \times 1\frac{3}{4}'' \times 29''$
MM	Waist door top rail	$\frac{3}{4}'' \times 3\frac{1}{8}'' \times 13\frac{1}{2}''$
NN	Waist door bottom rail	$\frac{3}{4}'' \times 3\frac{1}{2}'' \times 13\frac{1}{2}''$

HARDWARE

#0 Biscuits (2)

Offset hinges and mounting screws (2)

#8 × 1¼″ Flathead wood screws (16–20)

Door pull and catch

$10\frac{7}{8}'' \times 26\frac{1}{2}''$ Glass pane

Note: The glass pane must be cut to shape to fit the door. Most glass supply shops will be able to do this for you, but take the door frame in so they can fit the pane directly to the frame.

(continued)

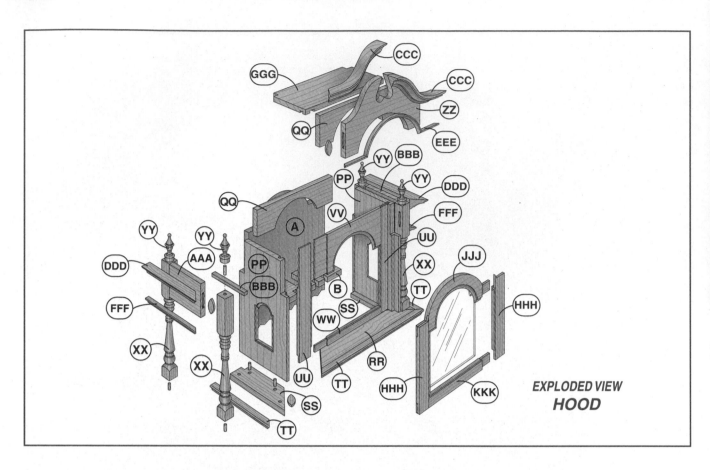

EXPLODED VIEW
HOOD

GRANDFATHER CLOCK ■ MATERIALS LIST (Finished Dimensions) — CONTINUED

PARTS — HOOD

PP	Hood sides (2)	$\frac{3}{4}'' \times 8\frac{1}{2}'' \times 18\frac{1}{4}''$
QQ	Hood top rails (2)	$\frac{3}{4}'' \times 5\frac{1}{2}'' \times 14\frac{1}{4}''$
RR	Hood frame front	$\frac{3}{4}'' \times 3'' \times 17\frac{1}{4}''$
SS	Hood frame sides (2)	$\frac{3}{4}'' \times 3'' \times 9\frac{1}{2}''$
TT	Hood frame molding (total)	$\frac{3}{4}'' \times 1'' \times 46''$
UU	Dial frame stiles (2)	$\frac{1}{4}'' \times 1\frac{7}{8}'' \times 17\frac{1}{2}''$
VV	Top dial frame rail	$\frac{1}{4}'' \times 6\frac{1}{4}'' \times 13\frac{1}{2}''$
WW	Bottom dial frame rail	$\frac{1}{4}'' \times 1\frac{1}{4}'' \times 13\frac{1}{2}''$
XX	Hood columns (4)	$1\frac{1}{2}'' \times 1\frac{1}{2}'' \times 18''$
YY	Finials (4)	$1\frac{1}{2}''$ dia.$'' \times 4\frac{3}{8}''$
ZZ	Scroll board	$\frac{3}{4}'' \times 10\frac{1}{2}'' \times 14\frac{1}{4}''$
AAA	Hood side aprons (2)	$\frac{3}{4}'' \times 5'' \times 5\frac{3}{4}''$
BBB	Apron spacers (2)	$\frac{3}{8}'' \times \frac{3}{4}'' \times 5\frac{3}{4}''$
CCC	Gooseneck moldings (2)	$1\frac{1}{2}'' \times 3\frac{9}{16}'' \times 12''$
DDD	Side top molding (total)	$1\frac{1}{2}'' \times 1\frac{3}{4}'' \times 24''$
EEE	Front door frame molding	$\frac{5}{8}'' \times 5'' \times 19''$
FFF	Side door frame molding (total)	$\frac{5}{8}'' \times \frac{3}{8}'' \times 24''$
GGG	Top	$\frac{3}{4}'' \times 6\frac{1}{2}'' \times 15\frac{3}{4}''$

HHH	Hood door stiles (2)	$\frac{3}{4}'' \times 1\frac{5}{8}'' \times 17\frac{1}{8}''$
JJJ	Hood door top rail	$\frac{3}{4}'' \times 5\frac{3}{4}'' \times 13\frac{1}{2}''$
KKK	Hood door bottom rail	$\frac{3}{4}'' \times 1\frac{1}{4}'' \times 13\frac{1}{2}''$

HARDWARE

#0 Biscuits (8)

$\frac{1}{4}''$ dia. $\times 1''$ dowels (12)

Knife hinges and mounting screws (2)

#8 $\times 1\frac{1}{4}''$ Flathead wood screws (16–20)

Door pull and catch

Westminster basic clockwork

RESOURCES

You can purchase the clockwork (#3260X), moon dial clock face (#7314C), and hands (#4930X) from:
Woodcraft Supply Corp.
P.O. Box 1686
Parkersburg, WV 26102-1686

How do I build it?

There's no getting around it; this is a complex project. To keep you from being overwhelmed, I'm going to try something completely different — I'm going to start with the final assembly! Look through the next 12 photos to get a sense of how this project goes together. Refer to these pages and the exploded views whenever you need to check how a portion of the clock fits together.

1 Fasten the bracket feet to the base frame.

2 Fasten the base frame to the bottom of the base case.

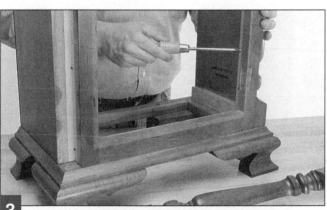

3 Attach the quarter columns to the base case, then lay the bottom and false bottom in place.

4 Attach the waist moldings to the waist case.

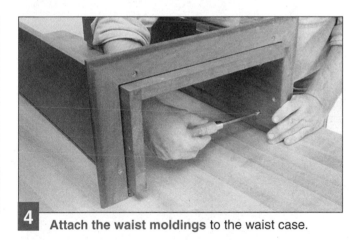

5 Secure the waist to the base, and install the waist and base doors.

6 Fasten the hood base to the bottom of the hood cabinet.

(continued)

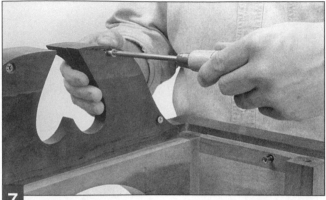

7   **Secure the gooseneck moldings** to the scroll board and side aprons.

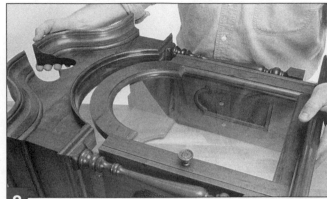

8   **Position the scroll board assembly** and door on the hood case.

9   **Fasten the scroll board assembly** to the hood case, and install the hood door.

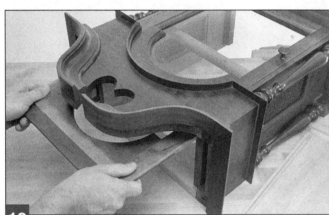

10   **Insert the dial frame** in the hood, and put the top in place.

11   **Attach the clock board** (with the clockwork mounted to it) to the waist and base cases.

12   **Slide the hood over** the clockwork and fasten it to the clock board. Place the finials on top of the columns.

GETTING STARTED

The key to any long undertaking like this is organization. Break the project up into several smaller assemblies, and build them one at a time.

THE PARTS OF THE CASE Jim divided the clock project into three assemblies — the *base, waist,* and *hood.* Each of these is a boxlike assembly with a door at the front. The boxes are stacked one on top of the other and are tied together by the back of the clock or the *clock board.*

MATERIALS Almost all of the parts are made from solid wood, except for clock board, the clock shelf, the bottom, and the false bottom in the base, which are made from plywood. The bottom, false bottom, and clock shelf can be made from ordinary cabinet-grade birch plywood, since these aren't visible on the assembled clock. But the clock board can be seen through the waist door. Consequently, the plywood veneer should match the wood used to build the clock. Jim made his clock from cherry and purchased cherry-veneer plywood for the clock board. As an alternative, you can use ordinary plywood and cover the waist section of the clock board with a veneer that matches the solid wood you use.

ATTACHING THE CLOCK TO THE CLOCK BOARD Before you do anything else, lay out the clock board as shown in the *Clock Board Layout* and the clock shelf. The shelf that Jim made is shown in the *Clock Shelf Layout,* but you may have to change the design to fit your clockwork. Join the clock board and the clock shelf, then attach the clockwork to them. This will give you a clear idea of the size of the works and the length and swing of the pendulum. Carefully measure these parts to make sure that the clockwork will fit the case you have planned. If necessary, adjust the size of the case.

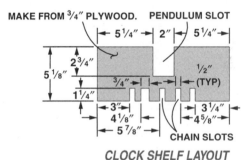

CLOCK SHELF LAYOUT

Fasten the clockwork to the clock board to check the size of the works and the swing of the pendulum. Also use this setup to adjust the works to keep the correct time. Temporarily fasten the clock board to a wall in a relatively *clean* room. (Don't keep it in your shop; dust will get in the works.) Attach the face and hands, then wind the clockwork. Carefully monitor the time it keeps against a timepiece you know keeps accurate time. Move the bob up or down the pendulum arm to make the clock run faster or slower, respectively.

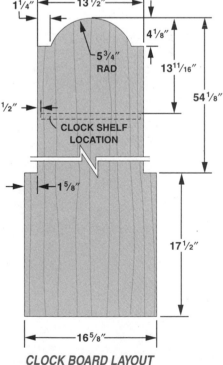

CLOCK BOARD LAYOUT

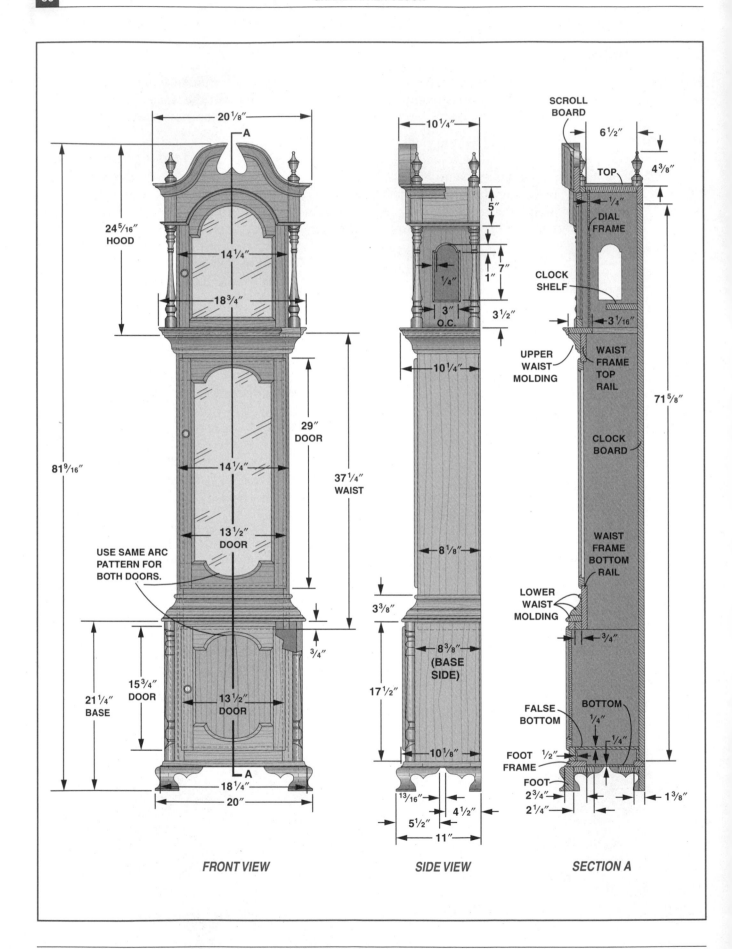

FRONT VIEW

SIDE VIEW

SECTION A

PLANNING YOUR ATTACK

As you get ready to dive into the woodworking, give some thought to the order in which you will build these assemblies. Jim strongly recommends that you tackle this clock from the ground up — base first, then the waist, and finally the hood. These assemblies are progressively more complex, allowing you to build your skills as you go.

MAKING THE BASE

Cut the parts of the base to size, except for the split columns and the feet. For the columns, glue up a turning block from two 1¼-inch-thick, 2½-inch-wide boards. Glue the boards face to face with kraft paper or wrapping paper between them. This will make the stock easier to split later on.

For the feet, cut three boards 1¾ inches thick × 3 inches wide and one ¾ inch thick × 3 inches wide. Join them to make a frame as shown in the *Foot Frame/Top View*. Miter the front corners, and rabbet the back. Reinforce the front corners with plywood splines.

JOINING THE CASE Cut rabbets in the *inside* faces of the base sides at the back edges. Then cut beads in the outside faces, as shown in the *Side Bead Detail* on page 66. Rabbet two arrises in each corner block so the rabbets are *diagonal* from one another, as shown in the *Base Corner Joinery Detail*, below left.

Join the front frame members with dowels. Then join the front frame, sides, corner blocks, side cleats, and side false bottom supports with screws. Glue the front cleat to the front frame rails. **Note: The bottoms are added later.**

CONSIDER THIS!

Most of the subassemblies in Jim's clock are screwed together rather than glued. This has several advantages. First, you can assemble the project without worrying about glue stains. Second, the project is easier to move and to handle because it can be taken apart. Finally — and most important — it's easier to finish. Because of the molded and turned shapes, there are lots of nooks and crannies in the assembled clock case. These make it difficult to apply, sand, and rub out a finish. But if you take the case apart, the nooks and crannies disappear.

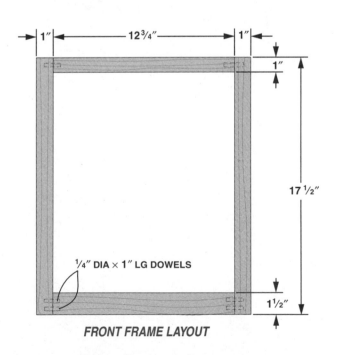

¼" × 3" × 1" SPLINE

12⅛"

10⅛"

1¾"

¾"

¾" WD × ¾" DP RABBET

10⅛"

TOP VIEW
FOOT FRAME

SIDE

#8 × 1¼" LG FHWS

¼" WD × ¼" DP RABBET

QUARTER COLUMN

CORNER BLOCK

½" WD × ½" DP RABBET

FRONT FRAME

BASE CORNER JOINERY DETAIL

1"

12¾"

1"

1"

17½"

¼" DIA × 1" LG DOWELS

1½"

FRONT FRAME LAYOUT

MAKING THE BASE FRAME Join the members of the base frame in much the same manner that you made the foot frame. Miter the front corners and butt the back corners, as shown in the *Base Frame Layout*. Reinforce the joints with splines, biscuits, or dowels, whichever you prefer.

Let the glue dry, then shape the front and side edges as shown in the *Base Frame Profile*. Join the complete base frame to the sides and front frame assembly with screws, using dowels for alignment. To do this, clamp the base frame to the bottom edges of the larger assembly. Drill through the bottom of the base frame and into the bottom edges of the sides and front frame rail. Take the assemblies apart, and glue dowels in the holes that you just drilled in the bottom edges of the sides and front frame. *Don't* glue them to the base frame. After the glue dries, insert the dowels in the holes in the base frame. Drive screws up through the base frame and into the sides and front frame.

Note: Jim went to the trouble of making mortises and tenons to join these assemblies, as shown in the photos on page 57. However, in hindsight, he admits this was over-building. Dowels are simpler, and they work just as well.

MAKING THE FEET The feet have an S-shaped profile on the sides and the front, as shown in the *Foot Pattern and Layout*. This is one of the few shapes that Jim didn't create with the router. Instead, he cut the concave part of the S-shape on a table saw, "coving" the front and side members of the foot frame. He created the convex portion with a hand plane, then cut the frame apart to create the individual feet.

Cut the foot patterns on a band saw, then glue blocks to the inside surfaces of the feet. These not only serve as glue blocks to reinforce the feet but also provide cleats to attach the feet to the base frame. Secure the feet to the frame with screws.

> **Look Here!** For more information on cutting cove molding, see page 104.

TRY THIS!

Certain hardwoods, such as cherry and maple, scorch easily during routing operations. If you let the bit dwell in one spot, even for a second, it will leave a burn mark. To prevent this, slow the bit speed. If you don't have a variable-speed machine, you can purchase a speed adjuster from most mail-order woodworking suppliers.

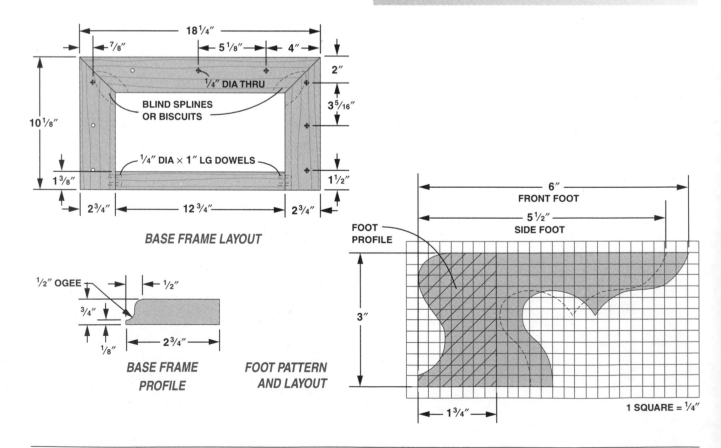

BASE FRAME LAYOUT

BASE FRAME PROFILE

FOOT PATTERN AND LAYOUT

1 SQUARE = 1/4"

METHODS OF WORK ■ *Making Bracket Feet*

The type of feet on Jim's clock are known as *bracket feet*. Each foot consists of two members joined at right angles to one another to form a bracket. Often, a bracket foot includes a glue block to reinforce the foot or a cleat to attach it to another assembly. When making a set of feet,

Jim starts by joining the foot stock to make a four-sided frame and then shapes the faces of the frame's front and sides. Later, he cuts the frame apart to make the individual brackets. This ensures that the wood grain and the profile are consistent from foot to foot.

1 To create the S-curve profile of the feet, begin by cutting a cove in the front and sides of the foot frame, near the bottom edges. Pass the frame over the 10-inch-diameter saw blade at a 22-degree angle to the blade, guiding it along a straightedge. Make the coves in several passes, cutting just 1/16 inch deep with each pass. For more information on cutting coves, see page 104.

2 Round-over the areas just above the cove to complete the S-shape. Use a hand plane to remove the stock, checking your work frequently with a template made from thin plywood or hardboard. **Tip: If you make bracket feet frequently, grind a scraper to a negative of the profile you want to cut. Use the scraper to cut the surface to its final shape once you get close with the plane.**

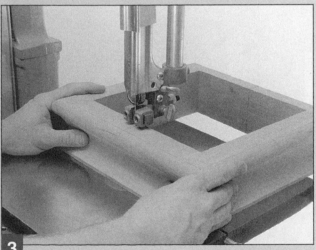

3 Cut the frame apart on a band saw to make four brackets. Lay out the shapes of the feet on the inside surfaces of the brackets.

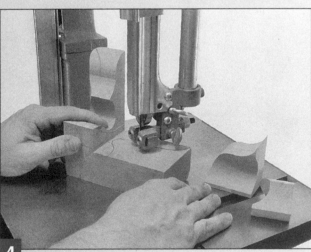

4 Cut the shapes of the feet with a band saw or a coping saw. Afterwards, sand the sawed edges smooth. Attach cleats and glue blocks as needed.

TURNING AND SPLITTING THE BASE COLUMN

The split column on the front corners of the base are actually *quartered* columns. To make these parts, first turn the column stock to the profile shown in the *Base Column Layout*. Sand and finish the turning on the lathe, then remove it and split it along the paper seam. Mount each half-column on a sheet of plywood, and rip them on the table saw to reduce them to quarters.

MAKING THE BASE DOOR

The doors on the clock are all frame-and-panel constructions — rails and stiles frame a wooden or a glass panel. The door frame members are joined at the corners with lap joints, while the panels rest in rabbets in the inside edges of the frame.

Additionally, the bottom two doors — the base and the waist door — are *lipped*. The door frames are rabbeted all around the perimeter to create a lip, and this lip overlays the door opening.

After turning the base column, position a chisel at the glue seam between the two halves. Align the cutting edge with the paper in the seam, and drive the chisel into the turning. The paper fibers will tear apart, and the column will separate cleanly at the seam.

Secure the split column to a sheet of plywood or hardboard with double-faced carpet tape. Guide the plywood along the fence, ripping the split column into two quarter-columns.

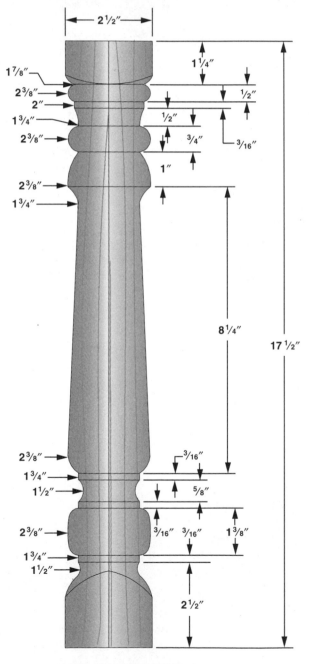

BASE COLUMN LAYOUT

Cut the joinery first, routing the lap joints on a router table. Then cut the profile of the frame member, as shown in the *Waist and Base Door Frame Profile*. Note that the roundovers on the top arrises are slightly different. The *inside* roundover has a slight step.

To fit the frame members together, you must remove this inside roundover from the rails and stile in the vicinity of the lap joints, as shown in the *Waist and Base Door Joinery Detail*. Miter the inside roundovers where they will join, and rip the unwanted section of the roundovers free from the frame members. When you fit the door frames together, rails and stiles should lap one another, but the molded inside edges should meet in a miter joint. Assemble the door frame with glue. Later, after the case is finished, mount the panel with small flathead wood screws.

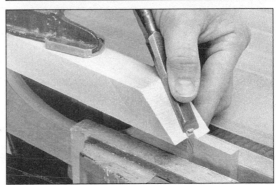

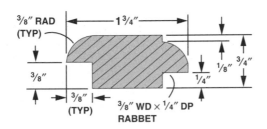

WAIST AND BASE DOOR FRAME PROFILE

To join the frame members, first rout lap joints *(top)*, then round and rabbet the edges to create the profile *(middle)*. Miter the inside molded edges where they meet *(bottom)*. Use an angled block as a chisel guide to make a perfect 45-degree miter.

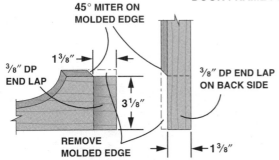

WAIST AND BASE DOOR JOINERY DETAIL

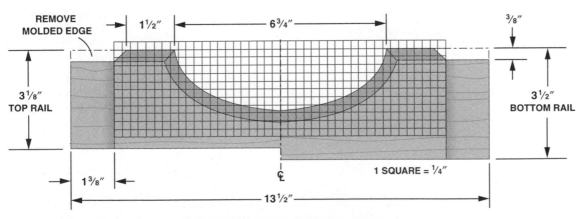

WAIST AND BASE DOOR RAIL LAYOUT

ADDING THE BOTTOMS That's right: bottoms *plural.* Jim put two bottoms in the base to create a secret compartment. The real bottom is just a simple board that rests on the base frame. The false bottom resides just above it, separated by two spacers. The top surface of the false bottom should be level with the top edge of the bottom front frame rail. Notch the corners of the false bottom to fit around the front corner blocks.

The false bottom simply rests over the real bottom in the base. To make it easily removable, attach a small ribbon to the back edge. Use the ribbon to help lift out the bottom.

MAKING THE WAIST

The waist in Jim's clock is simpler to construct than the base, but it's heavily decorated with moldings at the top and bottom of the assembly.

MAKE THE CASE The case is just four parts — the sides and the front rails. Rout mortises in the inside faces of the sides, as shown in the *Waist Side Layout,* then make matching tenons in the ends of the rails. Rabbet the inside back arrises of the sides and rout a bead on the outside arrises, as shown in the *Side Bead Detail.* Assemble the sides and rails with glue.

MAKE THE WAIST MOLDINGS Cut the profiles of the waist moldings on a router table. Note that the lower waist molding is "built up" from three smaller shapes, stacked one on top of the other. The upper molding is just a single shape. (See *Section A* on page 60.)

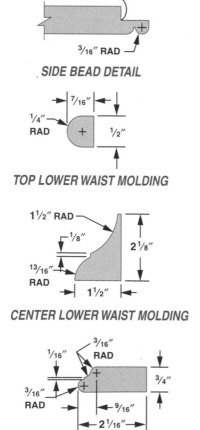

SIDE BEAD DETAIL

3/4" WD ×
3/8" DP RABBET
3/16" RAD

7/16"
1/4" RAD
1/2"

TOP LOWER WAIST MOLDING

1 1/2" RAD
1/8"
2 1/8"
13/16" RAD
1 1/2"

CENTER LOWER WAIST MOLDING

3/16" RAD
1/16"
3/16" RAD
3/4"
9/16"
2 1/16"

BOTTOM LOWER WAIST MOLDING

1 1/2"
1/2"
1 1/2" RAD
2 1/2"
5/8" RAD
3/16"

UPPER WAIST MOLDING

1/2"
1/4"
3"
3 1/2"

WAIST TENON DETAIL TOP

1/2"
1/4"
5"
5 1/2"

WAIST TENON DETAIL BOTTOM

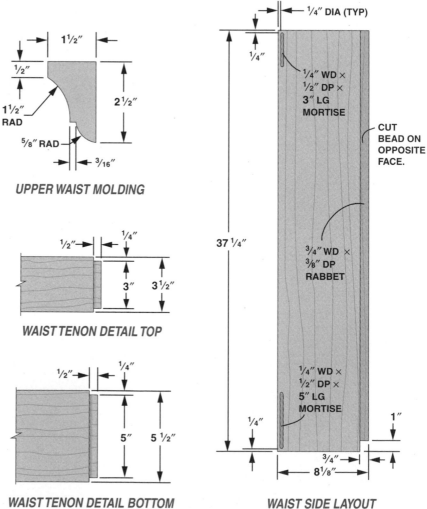

1/4" DIA (TYP)
1/4"
1/4" WD ×
1/2" DP ×
3" LG
MORTISE

CUT BEAD ON OPPOSITE FACE.

3/4" WD ×
3/8" DP RABBET

37 1/4"

1/4" WD ×
1/2" DP ×
5" LG
MORTISE

1/4"
1"
3/4"
8 1/8"

WAIST SIDE LAYOUT

METHODS OF WORK ■ *Routing Molded Shapes*

Cutting molded shapes is ordinarily a straight-forward routing operation, but there are a few tricks that may help.

■ If you must remove a great deal of stock to create the shape, make the molding in several passes, removing a little more stock with each pass.

■ Watch the grain direction, just as you do when planing and jointing. If the molding tends to chip or tear out as you cut it, you may be cutting "uphill," against the grain. Turn the board end for end to reverse the grain. If that doesn't solve the problem, try increasing the router speed or reducing the feed rate.

■ Don't attempt to rout slender stock. When making a narrow molding, start with a wide board. Shape the edge, then rip the narrow molding from the board on the table saw.

MAKING NARROW MOLDING

1 To make a narrow molding, start with a wide board. Rout the profile of the molding on the edge of the board. If you need a lot of molding, rout both edges. Warning: Never rout a slender piece of stock. It may break apart as you work.

2 Rip the molding free from the wide board on a table saw. If necessary, repeat until you've made all the molding stock you need.

MAKING CURVED MOLDING

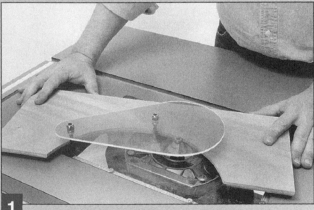

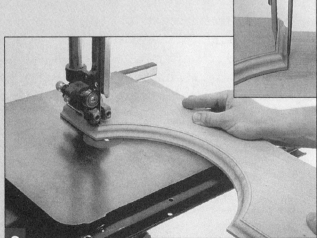

1 If you need a slender curved molding, the process is similar. Start with a wide board, and cut the inside curve of the molding in the edge. Sand the sawed edge, then shape it with a piloted router bit.

2 Using a compass as shown in the inset photo, scribe a line parallel to the curved edge. Cut the curved molding free of the board, following the line on a band saw.

QUICK FIXTURES ■ *Molding Aids*

LONG PUSHER

A long pusher helps you feed long, slender stock past a cutter. In some respects, this tool is similar to an ordinary pusher — it has a "heel" on the bottom edge that hooks over the end of a board to push it along. However, the bottom edge or "shoe" is elongated. This extra length enables you to hold the board down on the work table as you feed it along.

Make the pusher from ¾-inch plywood. The height of the tool should be at least 2 inches taller than the fence of your router table. This will let you push the stock without bumping your fingers on the fence.

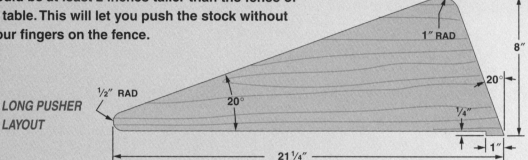

LONG PUSHER LAYOUT

½" RAD   1" RAD   8"   20°   20°   ¼"   1"   21¼"

FEATHERBOARD

A featherboard is another finger saver. The flexible fingers help to hold small or slender workpieces against a fence or work surface as you rout. Its fingers, or feathers, are set at an angle to reduce the risk of kickback.

To make a featherboard, cut multiple kerfs in the end of a hardwood board with a table saw or a band saw to create ⅛-inch-wide fingers. Use a clear hardwood with straight grain — maple and poplar are both good choices.

To use the featherboard, clamp it to a work surface or a fence so the fingers press against the work *ahead* of the blade or bit. The featherboard shown has a separate mount to help secure it even when you can't clamp it. Fasten the mount to any smooth surface with double-faced carpet tape, adjust the position of the featherboard on the mount so the fingers produce the necessary pressure, then lock it in place with roundhead wood screws.

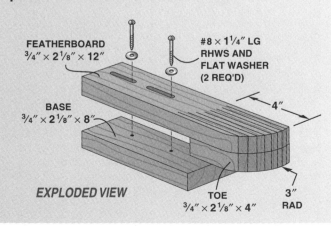

FEATHERBOARD
¾" × 2⅛" × 12"

#8 × 1¼" LG RHWS AND FLAT WASHER (2 REQ'D)

BASE
¾" × 2⅛" × 8"

4"

EXPLODED VIEW

TOE
¾" × 2⅛" × 4"

3" RAD

JOINING THE MOLDING The moldings wrap around the waist assembly on the front and sides. The parts are joined with a miter at the front corners.

To fit the moldings to the waist, first build up the lower waist molding stock. Stack the shapes and glue them face to face as shown in *Section A* on page 60. Let the glue dry completely, then fit the moldings to the case, mitering the adjoining ends.

Join the moldings at the miter joints with glue. If you wish, reinforce the joints with hidden splines or biscuits. However, don't glue the moldings to the case; glue only the miters. Let the glue dry, then screw the moldings to the case, driving the screws from inside the case and into the moldings.

MAKING THE WAIST DOOR Make the waist door exactly the same way you made the base door. Both doors are the same width, but the waist door is much higher. Cut the profiles of the rails as shown in the *Waist and Base Door Rail Layout* on page 65, then the lap joints that join the frame members, then the molded shapes of the rails and stiles. Miter the inside roundover where it meets at the corners.

TRY THIS!

When gluing up end-grain surfaces, as you do when assembling miter joints, the bond is much weaker than the glue bond between flat-grain surfaces. This is because the end grain wicks up a good deal of the glue before it sets, and the joint is partially "starved." To increase the strength of these joints, apply a thin coat of glue to the adjoining surfaces and let it sit for 15 or 20 minutes, then reapply the glue and clamp the parts together. The first coat of glue partially seals the end grain and prevents the second coat from being absorbed.

METHODS OF WORK ■ *Routing Spline Grooves*

Because miter joints are one of the weakest joints you can make, woodworkers often reinforce them with splines. The splines rest in grooves in the mitered ends of the adjoining boards. You can cut these grooves on a router table with a slot cutter.

1 **Secure the mitered board** to scraps of plywood with double-faced carpet tape so the mitered ends are even with one edge. One board will point toward the left side of the router table when you place the miter against the fence; the other will point toward the right. Start with the "left" miter. Position the stock on the table where you want to stop routing, and put a piece of tape on the fence. Make a mark even with the point of the miter. Turn on the router and feed the left-miter board into the cutter until the point is even with the mark.

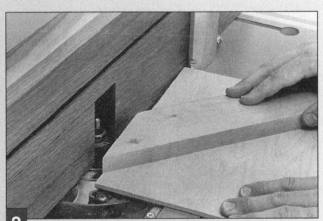

2 **For the right miter,** position the board where you want to *start* routing. Place a stop block against the back edge of the plywood, and clamp the block to the fence. Turn on the router, and brace the corner of the plywood against the stop block with the plywood cocked at a slight angle so the right-miter board doesn't quite touch the cutter. Slowly rotate the plywood and the board into the cutter, then feed it forward, past the cutter.

ATTACHING THE WAIST TO THE BASE Temporarily attach the clock board to the base. Rest the waist on the base, using the clock board to help position it side to side. Check that the back edges of the waist and base are flush, then drive screws horizontally through the waist sides and into the side cleats in the base.

MAKING THE HOOD

Now for the home stretch. The last assembly, the hood, is the most difficult (and the most rewarding) part of the clock project. Once again, cut the parts to size and carefully label them.

MAKE THE JOINERY Rout or cut the joints needed to assemble the hood case. This includes:

- The grooves, rabbets, and notches in the hood sides, as shown in the *Hood Side Layout*
- The lap joint that joins the members of the dial frame, as shown in the *Dial Frame Layout*
- The grooves, dadoes, and notches in the top, as shown in the *Hood Top Layout*

CUT THE PROFILES The hood rails, the scroll board, and the dial frame top rail all have arched profiles. Lay out these profiles and cut them with a band saw or saber saw. Also cut the arched soundholes in the hood sides with a scroll saw or coping saw. Using a roundover bit, round the inside edge of the soundholes and the dial frame members. Trim and miter the rounded edges of the frame members as you did when making the door. Carve the inside corners in the soundholes square to make the rounded shapes look as if they were applied molding joined by miters.

MAKE THE HOOD FRAME Miter the adjoining ends of the hood frame members and join them with splines or biscuits, as shown in the *Hood Frame Layout*. While the glue is drying on the frame, rout the hood frame molding profile. This is a *complex* shape; it will require at least two bits — an ogee and a roundover — to create the shape.

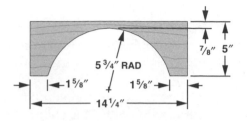

HOOD RAIL LAYOUT

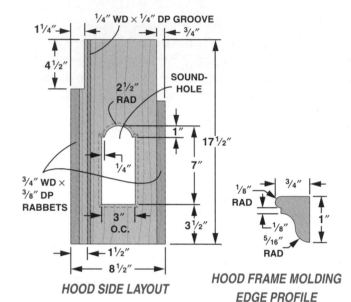

HOOD SIDE LAYOUT

HOOD FRAME MOLDING EDGE PROFILE

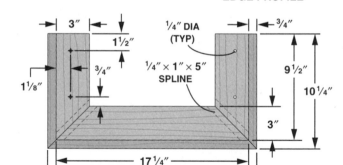

HOOD FRAME LAYOUT

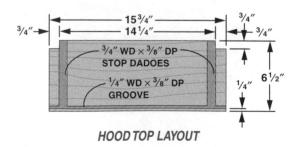

HOOD TOP LAYOUT

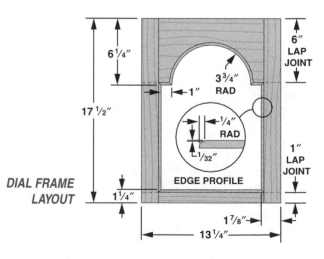

DIAL FRAME LAYOUT

Glue the hood frame molding to the hood frame, mitering the adjoining ends.

TURN THE HOOD COLUMNS AND FINIALS Turn the shapes of the hood columns and finials, as shown in the *Hood Column Layout* and the *Base Column Layout,* making four of each. Then drill round mortises in the bottom ends of the finial stock and both ends of the column stock.

ASSEMBLE THE BONNET Assemble the hood sides and back hood rail with screws to make the case. Glue the front hood rail to the scroll board. Also assemble the columns, hood side aprons, apron spacers, and scroll board with biscuits or dowels, gluing the parts together. This assembly forms a decorative curtain around the case.

Attach the hood frame to the bottom edge of the case in the same manner that you attached the base frame to the base. Clamp the frame to the case, and drill holes up through the frame and into the sides. Glue dowels in the stopped holes in the sides but not in the hood frame. Use these dowels to align the parts when assembling them. Fasten the frame to the case by driving screws up through the frame and into the sides.

Position the scroll board assembly around the case. Check that the back edges of the back columns are even with the back edges of the sides and that the front hood rail is resting in the front notches in the sides. Mark the location of the columns on the hood frame, and drill holes in the frame the same size as the mortises in the columns. Glue dowels in the bottom ends of the finials and columns. Insert the dowels in the frame holes, and secure the scroll board assembly by driving screws through the sides and into the apron spacers from inside the case.

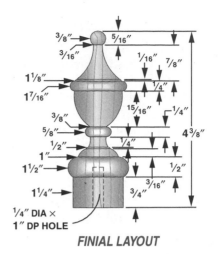

FINIAL LAYOUT

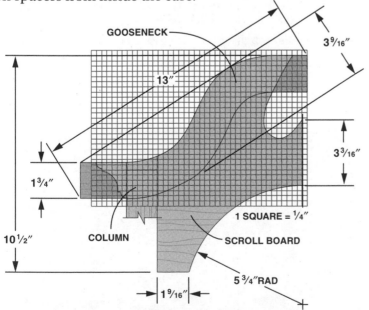

SCROLL BOARD AND GOOSENECK PATTERNS

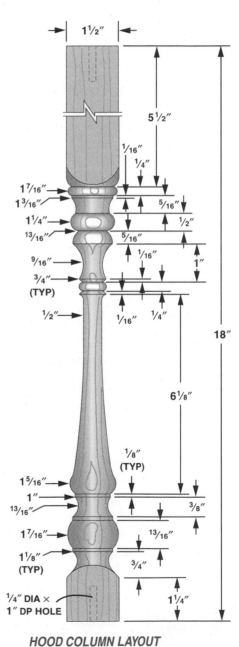

HOOD COLUMN LAYOUT

CREATING THE GOOSENECK MOLDING The top of the hood is adorned with an S-shaped molding known as a *gooseneck* molding, which wraps around the hood. The two S-shaped moldings are joined to straight pieces at the sides. Like the bracket feet, you can't create the cove in this molding with a router alone. You can, however, rough it out with a router and save a great deal of handwork.

Make each of the gooseneck moldings and the adjoining straight moldings in two parts — one 1¼ inches thick and the other ¼ inch thick, as shown in the *Gooseneck Molding Profile*. Starting

with a wide board, cut the inside curve of the gooseneck molding parts, and sand the sawed edges. Trace the cove profile on the ends of the thicker parts, and attach a roller guide to your router.

Using a roundnose bit, rough out the cove. Adjust the depth of cut and the position of the roller guide so you remove a small portion of the waste with each pass. As the profile emerges, smooth the surface with a scraper. When the profile is complete, rout a bead in the top edge. Also round-over the edge of the thinner part. Cut the *outside* curves of

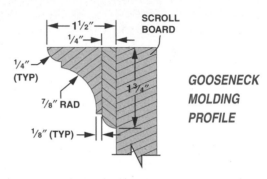

GOOSENECK MOLDING PROFILE

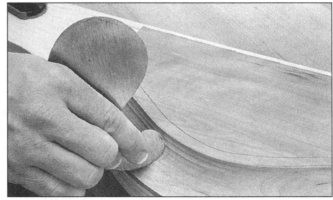

To create the gooseneck molding, rough out the shape of the cove with a roundnose bit. Mount a roller guide to the base of your router and use it to trace the contour of the gooseneck. With each pass, take a small bite, removing a little more of the waste.

After roughing out the cove, blend and smooth the surface with a round scraper. A "French curve" scraper *(shown)* works well for this task; so does an egg-shaped scraper. You can also grind a scraper to the precise profile you want to create.

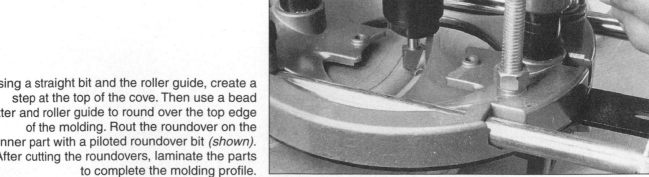

Using a straight bit and the roller guide, create a step at the top of the cove. Then use a bead cutter and roller guide to round over the top edge of the molding. Rout the roundover on the thinner part with a piloted roundover bit *(shown)*. After cutting the roundovers, laminate the parts to complete the molding profile.

the molding parts and glue them together. Later, miter the ends that will join the straight side moldings and attach them to the scroll board.

MAKING THE DOOR FRAME MOLDING Directly under the gooseneck moldings, a smaller molding traces the arch of the door opening then continues around the side of the hood. Create this arched molding using the method shown in "Routing Molded Shapes" on page 67. Cut the inside curve of the molding in a wide board, then rout the cut edge to make the molded shape. Afterwards, cut the outside curve to free the molding from the stock. Miter the moldings at the corners. Later, glue the front molding to the scroll board, but attach the side pieces to the aprons with screws.

MAKING THE HOOD DOOR Like the other doors on the clock case, the hood door frame has an arched rail, and the inside edges are shaped. However, this is an inset door, and as such, it has no lips around the outside edge. Make the frame in the same fashion as the other doors, joining the members with lap joints and mitering the rounded-over edges where they meet.

Mount this door on knife hinges. These hinges fasten to the top and bottom of the door. The advantage of knife hinges is that you can locate the pivot point wherever you need it simply by moving the hinges. On this project, the pivot should be at the outside right corner of the door. Mount the waist and base doors on offset hinges.

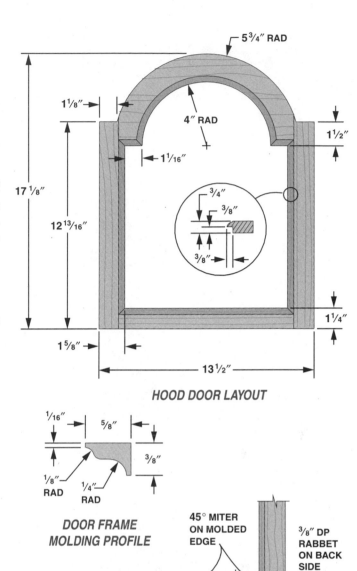

HOOD DOOR LAYOUT

DOOR FRAME MOLDING PROFILE

HOOD DOOR JOINERY DETAIL

TRY THIS!

When you install the glass in the doors (after the frames are finished), use a thin bead of silicone caulk to secure the glass in the rabbets. This is much easier than using traditional glazing points.

FINISHING THE CLOCK

To finish the clock case, take it apart completely, removing most of the screws. Apply a durable finish to all wooden surfaces, inside and out. Although some craftsmen disagree, Jim and I feel that finishing the inside and outside of a case with an equal number of coats makes the assembly more stable. All of the wooden surfaces absorb and release moisture at the same rate. Rub out the finish *and* wax all exterior surfaces before reassembling the clock.

Cut shallow mortises for the knife hinges in the top and bottom of the hood door frame and the inside surfaces of the door opening. You have to take the hood partially apart to cut the mortise and install the hinges.

Loaves and Fishes Display Shelves

In this chapter...

PRACTICAL KNOW-HOW

Standard Shelving Dimensions	76
Pattern-Routing Techniques	83
Pin Routing	84

JIGS AND FIXTURES

Alignment Gauge	80
Pin-Routing Attachment	85

SHOP SOLUTIONS

Detail Sanding with a Saber Saw	87

The sides of this shelf unit have decorative cutouts called *openwork*. In openwork, the wood is pierced clear through. The openings and the *bridges* between them form a pleasing pattern.

Most craftsmen don't think of a router as a tool for creating openwork. It's more common to do it with a scroll saw or saber saw, as Scott Harrold, the guest craftsman who made these shelves, points out. But Scott also knows the router is an excellent tool for openwork, particularly if the decorative pattern is made up of repeating elements. It's much easier and you get better results if you cut one or more templates and *pattern-rout* the openwork than it is to lay it all out and make the cutouts with a saw.

We'll get into pattern routing in just a bit. We have a few things to consider before we get there, and first off is the size of the shelving unit.

What size should it be?

Like any storage unit, the size of a set of shelves depends on what you want to store on them. But that's only *one* of your considerations.

SHELVING DIMENSIONS When building shelves, you must decide on the *depth* of the shelves, the *spacing* between them, the shelving *span*, the *height* of the shelves, and the overall *height* of the unit.

Depth. The depth of the shelves is determined by not only the size of the items you will keep on the shelves but also whether the shelves will stand on the floor or hang on the wall. As a general rule of thumb, hanging units aren't as deep as standing

You can sidestep the whole question of shelf spacing by making *adjustable* shelves with movable supports. The most common and perhaps the easiest to install are shelving support pins, shown here. Unfortunately, adjustable shelves aren't appropriate for every shelving design. Mary Jane decided on fixed shelves when she designed the loaves-and-fishes display shelves because she didn't want to see the ends of the shelves through the openwork.

DESIGN SAVVY

There are several simple mathematical techniques for spacing shelves in an aesthetically pleasing manner. The simplest is an *arithmetic progression.* If the space between the top shelves is 8 inches, make the next space down 10 inches, then 12 inches, and so on, adding 2 inches to each space. You might also consider a *geometric progression,* increasing each space by a constant ratio. Starting out with an 8-inch space, multiply by a ratio of 1¼, making the next space 10 inches. Multiply by 1¼ again, and the next space becomes 12½ inches.

units. Narrower shelves limit the stress on the joinery and the fasteners that hold them to the wall.

Spacing. The spacing between shelves depends on not just the size of the items stored but also the position of the shelves in the unit. Traditionally, furniture designers put the largest spaces at the bottom of a unit and the smallest at the top. If you build it the other way around, the shelves look top-heavy.

Shelf Height. The heights of the top and bottom shelves are determined by ergonomics. What can you comfortably reach? On the average, the highest shelf in a unit shouldn't be more than 72 to 78 inches above the floor. The lowest shelves should be a few inches above the floor in a standing unit and no lower than waist level in a hanging unit.

Span. The span of the shelves depends on not only the width that you want to make the shelving unit, but also the material you're building with. Different materials — and different thicknesses of materials — have different strengths. Consequently, they begin to sag at different spans. Particleboard has the least strength, followed by plywood. Solid wood has the most strength.

Overall Height. The height of the unit itself is determined by the level of the top shelf, the spacing of the top shelf, and whether the unit stands or hangs. It can be anywhere from 24 inches high clear to the ceiling.

SPECIAL CONSIDERATIONS When sizing openwork shelves, there are some special considerations you'll need to think through. The most important is that the openwork reduces the strength of the unit sides, and the shelves may not support heavy items. For that reason, Mary Jane designed this project as a display for collectibles. Unless you collect boat anchors or airplane engines, this design should work fine for you.

If you wanted to make openwork shelves to store something heavier, there are two ways to go. First, consider making the sides from a void-free material, such as marine plywood or Baltic Birch plywood. This would make the plies visible, but you might disguise them by staining or painting the edges of the openings. Second, reduce the size of the openings to make the bridges wider. You won't remove as much stock when you rout the openwork; consequently you won't lose as much strength.

OOPS!

If you make ceiling-high shelves, make the unit in two parts. This has nothing to do with making the unit easier to move; it has to do with standing the unit up in place. True story — I once built a ceiling-high china cupboard in one piece. It was a handsome piece, but when I tried to stand it up in the room I had made it for, it wouldn't fit. It wasn't too tall; the corners scraped the ceiling as I raised the unit. Eventually, I had to remove part of the ceiling in order to install the cupboard.

You'll also need to consider the shelf spacing in relation to the design. In Mary Jane's design, the shelves are all spaced evenly because the elements in the loaves-and-fishes design are all the same size. This is a no-no in some schools of furniture design, but it seems to work well enough here. It's just one of the many tradeoffs you sometimes have to make when thinking through a project. If we had wanted to make a unit with progressively spaced shelves, we would have needed a different pattern for the openwork.

STANDARD SHELVING DIMENSIONS

The size of a shelving unit depends on many factors — what you have to store, the shelving materials, and whether the unit hangs on the wall or rests on the floor. These measurements are intended as guidelines only.

Depth of Shelves

Small or narrow objects	6"–8"
Books or large objects	10"–12"
Dishes (hanging unit)	12"–13"
Linens, clothes	15"–18"
Audio components	18"–20"
Video components	18"–24"
Pots and pans (standing unit)	24"–25"

Shelf Spacing

Small objects, paperback books	7"–8"
Medium objects, hardcover books	10"–12"
Large objects, tall books	13"–15"

Shelf Height

Highest shelf	72"–78" above floor
Lowest shelf (standing unit)	3"–4" above floor
Lowest shelf (hanging unit)	36"–54" above floor

Maximum Shelving Span (20 lb. per foot)

¾"-thick particleboard	24"
¾"-thick plywood	30"
¾"-thick softwood	36"
¾"-thick hardwood	48"
1"-thick softwood	48"
1"-thick hardwood	54"

Overall Height

Standing unit	24"–84"
Hanging unit	24"–42"

What style will it be?

The loaves-and-fishes openwork design was adapted from a Gothic design technique known as *arcading*. These geometric designs, used in both architecture and furniture, were laid out with simple arithmetic — there were no artistic skills necessary. Often, these designs also included some religious symbolism. The loaves and fishes, for example, are a geometrical representation of the miracle of the loaves and fishes from the New Testament — the large circle is a basket of fishes; the long, tapered shapes are loaves of bread.

Gothic arcading is just one of many possibilities for openwork. Shown below are two more.

FRETWORK STYLE

Intricately pierced designs in wood became popular with the invention of the fretsaw in the seventeenth century. Fretwork became all the rage in Victorian times with the invention of mechanical scroll saws, and electric power gave it another boost in this century. *Fretwork* is commonly done using scroll saws — the delicate shelf shown is a scroll saw project. But you can adapt many fretwork designs for the router. Because you are limited by the sizes of the router bit and guide collar, you can't do extremely intricate work. But the router gives you a decided advantage when cutting larger patterns with repetitive elements.

SOUTHWEST "MUDEJAR" STYLE

When the Spanish conquered the U.S. Southwest, they brought with them a unique blend of European and African furniture forms. One of the most striking was a decorative method derived from the Moorish design tradition, the *mudejar*. (The African Moors ruled Spain during medieval times.) These geometric designs could be painted, carved, or pierced. The openwork panels in this Southwest cupboard are one example.

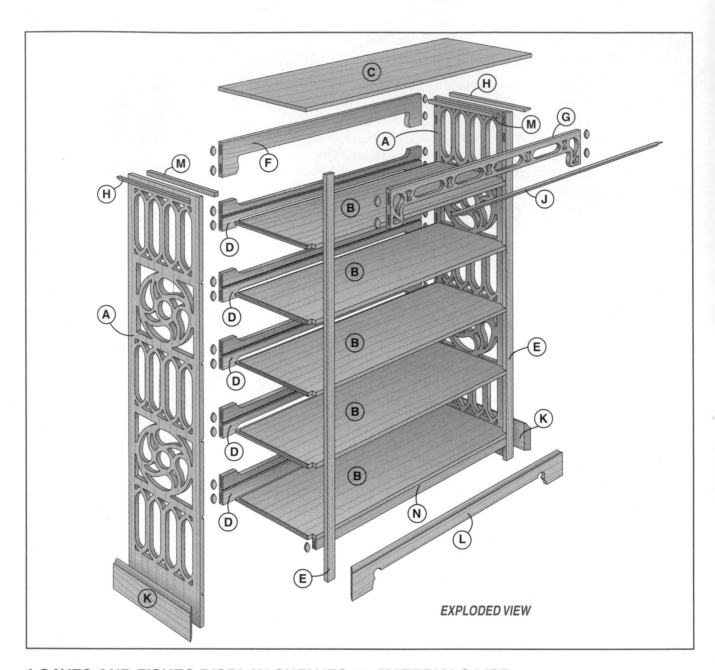

EXPLODED VIEW

LOAVES AND FISHES DISPLAY SHELVES ■ *MATERIALS LIST* (Finished Dimensions)

PARTS

A	Sides (2)	$\frac{1}{2}'' \times 11\frac{1}{2}'' \times 59''$
B	Shelves (5)	$\frac{1}{2}'' \times 11\frac{3}{4}'' \times 32\frac{1}{2}''$
C	Top	$\frac{1}{2}'' \times 13'' \times 35\frac{5}{8}''$
D	Back braces (5)	$\frac{1}{2}'' \times 4\frac{1}{2}'' \times 32''$
E	Stiles (2)	$\frac{1}{2}'' \times 1'' \times 59''$
F	Back valance	$\frac{1}{2}'' \times 5'' \times 32''$
G	Front valance	$\frac{1}{2}'' \times 5'' \times 31''$
H	Top side moldings (2)	$\frac{1}{2}'' \times \frac{1}{2}'' \times 12\frac{1}{2}''$
J	Top front molding	$\frac{1}{2}'' \times \frac{1}{2}'' \times 34''$

K	Bottom side moldings (2)	$\frac{1}{2}'' \times 4'' \times 12\frac{1}{2}''$
L	Bottom front molding	$\frac{1}{2}'' \times 4'' \times 34''$
M	Cleats (2)	$\frac{1}{2}'' \times \frac{1}{2}'' \times 11''$
N	Bottom cleat	$\frac{1}{2}'' \times 1\frac{1}{2}'' \times 31''$

HARDWARE

#6 × ¾" Roundhead wood screws (12)

#6 Flat washers (12)

#00 Biscuits (30)

How do I build it?

The shelves are designed to look delicate. Not only does the openwork reduce the perceived mass of the piece, the materials themselves are thinner than you'd normally use. Because of this, it's essential that you use good stock and prepare it properly.

PREPARING THE MATERIALS

Scott's first instinct when he saw Mary Jane's design was to make the sides of the shelves from plywood. This would strengthen the bridges in the openwork and make them less likely to split or break as he routed the patterns. (Plywood, in fact, was invented in the early nineteenth century by John Henry Belter just for delicate openwork in Victorian Rococo Revival furniture.) But after some thought, he decided to try a solid wood. He chose poplar because it machines easily and has little tendency to chip or split. Walnut, cherry, maple, and mahogany are also good candidates.

SHOP SAVVY

When cutting intricate patterns in solid wood, use stock with as straight a grain as you can find.

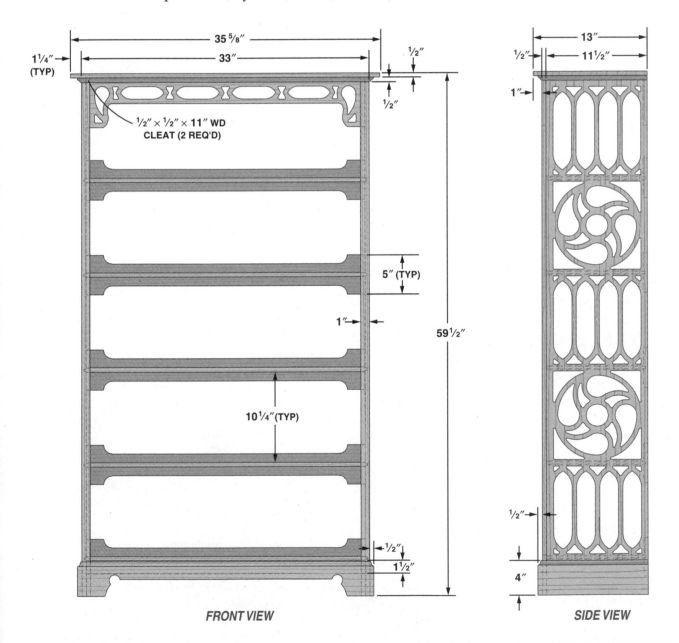

FRONT VIEW *SIDE VIEW*

Bring the lumber into the shop and let it shop dry for a week or more. This gives the moisture content in the wood a chance to adjust to the relative humidity in your shop and stabilize. Then plane all the stock down to a thickness of ½ inch.

CUTTING THE JOINERY

The joinery in this project is a bit more involved than you would ordinarily find in a set of shelves. The shelves join the sides and the back braces with tongue-and-dado joints. Ordinarily, you might use simple dadoes, but the tongue-and-dado combination adds strength to the delicate structure.

Rout grooves in the back braces as shown in the *Back Brace Layout,* and dadoes in the sides as shown in the *Side Joinery Layout.* Create the

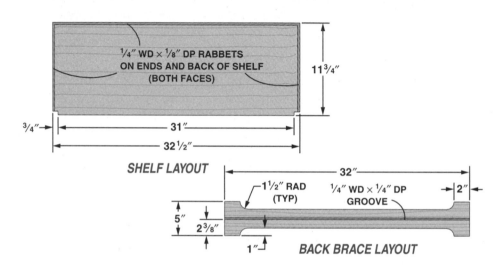

¹/₄″ WD × ¹/₈″ DP RABBETS ON ENDS AND BACK OF SHELF (BOTH FACES)

11³/₄″

³/₄″   31″   32¹/₂″

SHELF LAYOUT

—1¹/₂″ RAD (TYP) ¹/₄″ WD × ¹/₄″ DP GROOVE 32″ 2″

5″ 2³/₈″ 1″

BACK BRACE LAYOUT

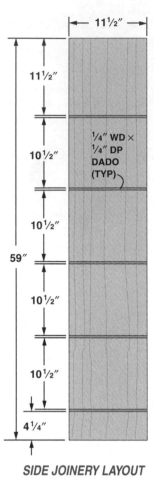

11½″

11½″

¹/₄″ WD × ¹/₄″ DP DADO (TYP)

10½″

10½″

59″

10½″

10½″

10½″

4¹/₄″

SIDE JOINERY LAYOUT

TRY THIS!

Rout the dadoes in the side with the Dado-and-Rabbet Jig shown on page 17. To help position the sides for each cut, make a simple gauge.

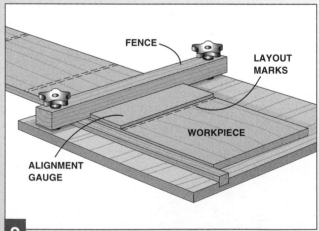

FENCE

LAYOUT MARKS

WORKPIECE

ALIGNMENT GAUGE

1   **To make the gauge,** place a thin 6-inch-wide piece of hardboard or plywood against the jig fence, securing it to a scrap with double-faced carpet tape. Mount the ¼-inch straight bit you'll use to cut the dadoes in your router. Guide the router along the fence, cutting through the hardboard.

2   **To use the gauge,** first place the workpiece in the jig, under the fence. Butt one edge of the gauge against the fence, align the other edge with the layout marks for the dado, and tighten the knobs. The work will be correctly positioned for routing.

tongues on the shelves by rabbeting the ends and the back edges on both faces, as shown in the *Shelf Layout*. Also notch the front corners of the shelves to fit around the stiles.

ROUTING DECORATIVE PATTERNS

Once you've cut the joinery, it's time to rout the openwork. Technically, the routing technique used to do this is *pattern routing*. There's nothing to this that I haven't demonstrated already — just follow a template with your router. It's similar to the procedure used to make the dovetails in the Mule Chest (page 18) or the mortises in the Writing Table (page 39). The only difference is the results — you get a decorative pattern instead of joinery.

MAKING THE TEMPLATES To create the patterns, first make the templates for the basket of fishes, the loaves, and the valance. The patterns below are half-sized; photocopy them, enlarging them to 200 percent. Adhere the full-sized copies to ½-inch plywood with spray adhesive. Cut out the openings with a scroll saw or saber saw, then sand the cut edges as smooth as possible.

Note that the openings in the templates are slightly larger than the cutouts you want to rout in the work. This compensates for the difference in diameters between the router bit and the guide collar.

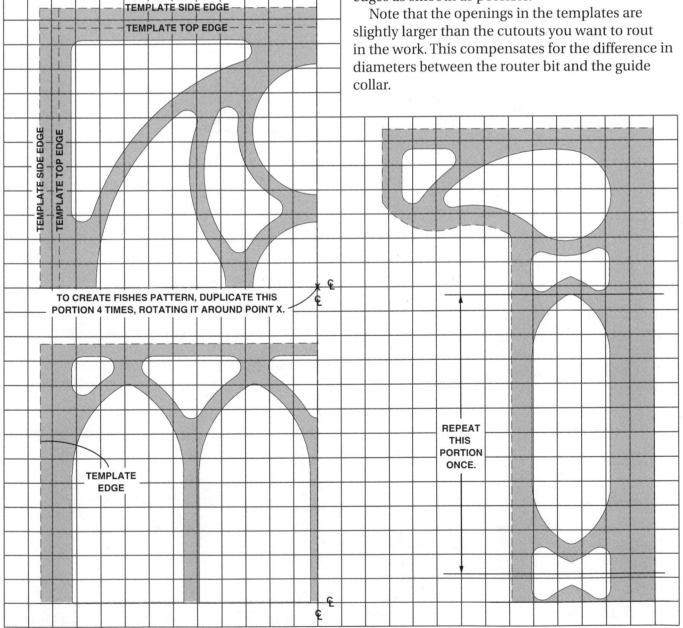

TEMPLATE SIDE EDGE
TEMPLATE TOP EDGE
TEMPLATE SIDE EDGE
TEMPLATE TOP EDGE
TO CREATE FISHES PATTERN, DUPLICATE THIS PORTION 4 TIMES, ROTATING IT AROUND POINT X.
TEMPLATE EDGE
REPEAT THIS PORTION ONCE.

1 SQUARE = ½"

TEMPLATE PATTERNS

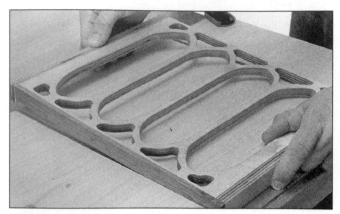

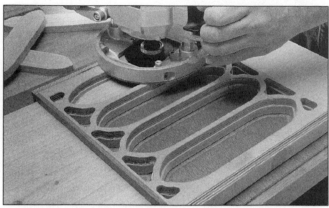

The most critical step in pattern routing is positioning the template — especially if you are cutting a repeating pattern. To aid in positioning the loaves and fishes templates, Scott carefully sized them and attached cleats to two edges. One cleat hooked over the back edge of the side; the other fit in the dadoes.

Once the templates are positioned and secured, rout the patterns, following the edges of the templates. Since you'll be cutting completely through the work, secure it to a scrap of plywood or particleboard to back up the cut and protect your bench top.

ROUTING THE CUTOUTS Although you don't have to draw the complete pattern of cutouts on the work, you must carefully measure the work and mark it so you can position the templates properly. To rout the cutouts in the sides, Scott made the templates so he could align the template edges with the back edges of the sides and the dadoes as references. The valance template was made to be aligned with the ends and top edge of the valance. This greatly simplified the layout chores.

Once you have aligned the template, secure it to the work with double-faced carpet tape. If you aren't as enamored of this stuff as we are, you can make the templates about 10 inches longer than needed on one side. This will give you enough extra stock to clamp them to the work without interfering with the movement of the router.

Mount a ¼-inch straight bit in the router, and fasten a ⁷⁄₁₆-inch guide collar to the baseplate of your router. Make sure the bit is centered in the collar. Adjust the depth of cut to bite just ⅛ inch into the

stock, and rout the pattern, following the inside edges of the template with the guide collar. Rout the entire pattern, readjust the depth of cut to bite a little deeper, and continue until you cut completely through the work. Reposition the template — or change to another template — and do it again.

MAKING THE VALANCE, BRACES, AND MOLDINGS

Remove the guide collar and switch to an ogee bit. Shape the top edges of the bottom molding. Make the slender top moldings by shaping the edge of a wide board, then ripping the moldings free on a table saw.

Lay out the profiles of the valances, back braces, and bottom front molding, as shown in the *Back Brace Layout, Template Patterns,* and *Bottom Molding Detail.* Cut the profiles with a band saw or saber saw, and sand the cut edges smooth.

SAFEGUARD

When small parts break free inside the pattern, the router bit may kick them out with tremendous force. To eliminate this danger, either (1) adhere the work to the backup board with double-faced carpet tape, or (2) cut away all the waste inside the template openings — don't just trace the outlines with the bit.

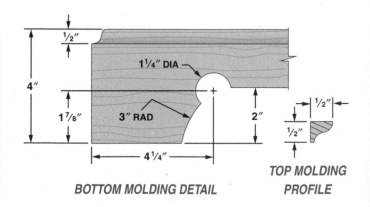

BOTTOM MOLDING DETAIL

TOP MOLDING PROFILE

SHOP SAVVY ■ *Pattern-Routing Techniques*

There are three common pattern-routing techniques, each using a different bit and a different setup. Which one is best? That depends on your preferences and the work you have to do.

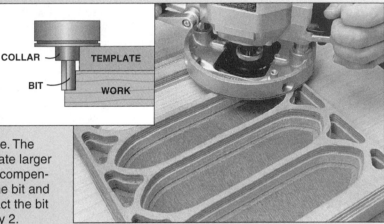

Use a *straight bit* to cut the pattern and a *guide collar* to follow the template. The advantage of this method is that there are many different diameters of bits and collars to choose from. This, in turn, gives you a great deal of flexibility in designing the template. The disadvantage is that you must make the template larger or smaller than the pattern your want to cut to compensate for the difference in diameters between the bit and the collar. How much larger or smaller? Subtract the bit diameter from the collar diameter and divide by 2.

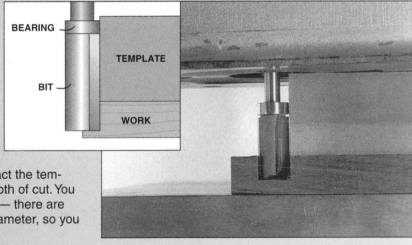

Use a *pattern-routing bit* to follow a template. This bit has a "top" bearing that rests on top of the cutting flutes, between the head and the shaft. The bearing is the same diameter as the cutter; consequently you can make your template the same size as the pattern you want to create. To rout thick stock, however, the template must be at least as thick as the cutting flutes are long — otherwise the bearing won't contact the template on the first pass. This limits your depth of cut. You are also limited by the available bit sizes — there are no pattern-routing bits under ½ inch in diameter, so you can't rout the openings smaller than that.

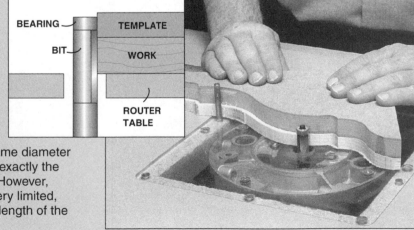

Use a *flush-trim bit* in a table-mounted router to follow a template. A flush-trim bit has a pilot bearing at the end of the cutting flutes. Cut away most of the waste from the work with a band saw or saber saw, then attach the template to it. Adjust the depth of cut so the bearing rests against the edge of the template and the flutes bite into the work. Because the pilot bearing is the same diameter as the cutter, the bit will trim the work to exactly the same profile or pattern as the template. However, the available diameter of the cutters is very limited, and the work can be no thicker than the length of the cutting flutes.

ANOTHER WAY TO GO ■ *Pin Routing*

You can also create a pattern by guiding a template against a stationary pin. This is called *pin routing.* The template is attached to your work. As you guide the template against the pin, it moves the work over a bit. Ordinarily, the bit and the pin are the same diameter, so you can make the template the same size as the pattern to be cut. But you can also use bits of different diameters — even bits that cut decorative shapes, so long as they *don't* have a pilot bearing *and do* have "top-cut" or "point-cut" flutes. (A straight bit is a typical top-cut bit; a V-bit is a point-cut bit.)

1 **To align the pin** perfectly with the bit, use the bit to bore a round mortise for the pin in the end of the pin holder. Draw a line along the length of the pin holder, and insert the holder in the beam. Draw a mark on the beam next to the line on the pin holder. Whenever you insert the holder in the beam, or move the holder up and down, the line must be aligned with the mark. Adjust the depth of cut so the router bit is below the surface of the router table. Lower the beam until the end of the holder touches the table above the bit. Turn on the router and raise it slowly, boring a mortise in the end of the holder. Remove the holder, and secure a pin in the mortise with epoxy.

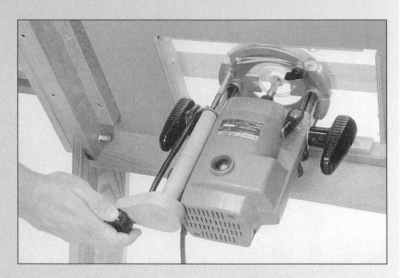

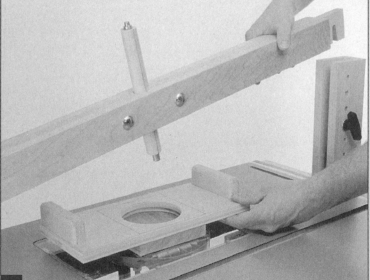

2 **Adjust the depth of cut** so the bit bites just ⅛ inch into the work. Drill a hole slightly larger than the bit in the waste area in the work. Attach the template to the work with double-faced carpet tape. If you're routing a small piece, make the template larger — this will give you some "handles" to hang on to. Place the work and the template over the bit with the bit sticking up in the hole you drilled. Lower the pin until it's slightly below the top surface of the template.

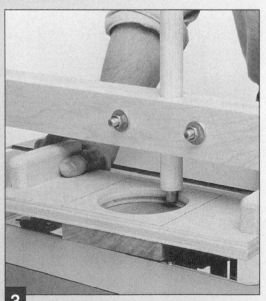

3 **Turn on the router** and move the work over the bit, keeping the template pressed against the pin. After tracing the template, readjust the depth of cut to bite a little deeper and repeat. Continue until you have cut the pattern as deep as you want.

QUICK FIXTURE ■ *Pin-Routing Attachment*

To convert your router table to a pin router, make a simple frame to hold a guide pin directly above the bit on a router table. From ¾-inch-thick hardwood, glue up two U-shaped vertical supports and a horizontal beam that stretches between them. Screw the supports to the edges of the router table so the beam crosses over the router. Make a pin holder from hardwood dowel stock, and mount it directly over the router bit. The center of the pin holder must be aligned as well as possible with the axis of the router bit. Use the router bit itself to bore the mortise in the holder for the pin — this will ensure that the pin is perfectly centered above the bit.

To use the attachment, first attach a template to the work. With the work resting on the router table, adjust the beam so it's no more than an inch above the template. (The greater the distance above the template, the more chance there is that the pin will be deflected sideways as you guide the template against it. This, in turn, will alter the pattern you're trying to rout.) Once the beam is positioned, adjust the height of the pin holder so the pin rests beside the template. Tighten the knob to lock both the beam and the pin holder in place before you rout. To raise the pin, either to move it to another part of the template or to remove the work, loosen one end of the beam and swing it up.

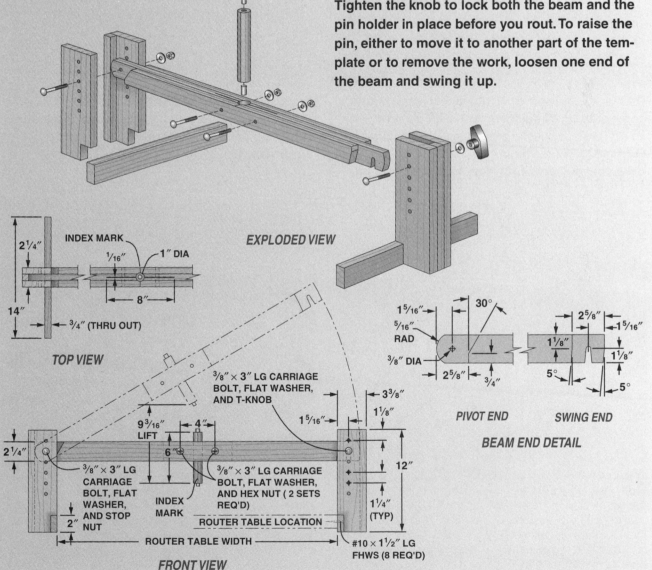

EXPLODED VIEW

TOP VIEW

INDEX MARK

2¼"

14"

1/16"

1" DIA

8"

¾" (THRU OUT)

FRONT VIEW

9³/₁₆" LIFT

4"

6"

2¼"

2"

⅜" × 3" LG CARRIAGE BOLT, FLAT WASHER, AND STOP NUT

INDEX MARK

⅜" × 3" LG CARRIAGE BOLT, FLAT WASHER, AND HEX NUT (2 SETS REQ'D)

⅜" × 3" LG CARRIAGE BOLT, FLAT WASHER, AND T-KNOB

ROUTER TABLE LOCATION

ROUTER TABLE WIDTH

1⁵/₁₆"

3⅜"

1⅛"

12"

1¼" (TYP)

#10 × 1½" LG FHWS (8 REQ'D)

BEAM END DETAIL

PIVOT END

1⁵/₁₆"

5/16" RAD

⅜" DIA

2⅝"

¾"

30°

SWING END

2⅝"

1⁵/₁₆"

1⅛"

1⅛"

5°

5°

ASSEMBLING THE SHELVES

There are just two more pieces to join, and you have your choice of joinery. You must join the back valance to the sides and the front valance to the stiles to make a face frame. Scott did this with biscuits, but you can use dowels or splines.

Once all the joinery is cut, finish sand the parts. This can be quite a chore, especially when it comes time to sand the routed edges of the openwork. However, there are a few tips on page 87 to help cut this chore down to size.

Once the parts are sanded, glue the shelves to the back braces and assemble the face frame with glue. Let the glue dry, then attach the shelf assemblies and the back valance to the sides with glue. Add the bottom cleat beneath the bottom shelf. Then glue the face frame to the front edges of the sides and the bottom cleat.

Drill ¼-inch-diameter holes in the cleats for the screws that will attach the top. Note that these holes are slightly larger than the shanks of the screws — this allows the top to expand and contract. Screw the cleats to the inside faces of the sides, flush with the top ends.

Cut the molding to fit around the sides and front of the assembly, mitering the adjoining ends. Attach the front moldings with glue, but secure the top side moldings with brads and the bottom side moldings with roundhead screws in oversized holes. Both arrangements allow the sides to expand and contract. (The brads bend slightly as the wood moves.) Drive the screws from the inside surfaces of the sides so you won't see them on the assembled pieces. Also, attach the top by driving screws up through the cleats.

TRY THIS!

On the shelves shown, Scott accented the edges of the cutouts by painting them with black acrylic paint. This has several advantages. If the router left burn marks when you routed the patterns, the black paint covers them neatly. You don't have to sand and sand to get them out. If you've used plywood to make the sides, the paint disguises the plies. And finally, the paint emphasizes the openwork, making the design pop.

1 **Paint the edges of the cutouts** in the sides and the front valance. before you assemble the shelves, using black acrylic paint. Don't bother masking the faces of the workpieces, and don't worry if you accidentally brush some paint on the faces. *Don't* wipe the errant paint off, just let it dry.

2 **When the paint has dried** completely, sand the faces to remove any paint on them. After sanding, assemble the shelves. If you think the paint might react with the finish you want to use, seal it with a thin coat of shellac before applying the finish.

SHOP SAVVY ■ *Saber Saw Sanding*

While you're teaching your router new tricks, you might also try something new with your saber saw. With a little ingenuity, a saber saw can make an effective detail sander. The only hitch to this trick is that you must have a *variable-speed saw,* capable of low speeds. Regular saws run too fast to be used for sanding.

1 **Grind or file the teeth** off a used saber saw blade. The blade should be pretty thick. Because you'll be putting sideways pressure on the blade, you don't want to use a slender scrolling blade.

2 **The blade is too hard** to be used by itself as a sanding platen. To create a surface with some give, wrap a thin piece of leather around the blade and secure it with epoxy. Also make an auxiliary sole from a thin piece of hardboard. When using the saber saw to sand, fasten this to the metal sole with double-faced carpet tape. This will prevent the metal sole from marring the work.

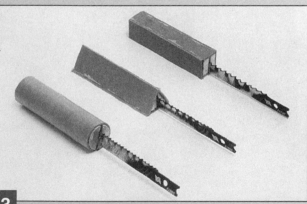

3 **If you need sanding shapes** other than a simple flat blade, fashion them from hardwood. Cut a slot in the blade large enough to insert a saber saw blade and epoxy the blade in the slot. Cover the wooden shape with leather. **Note: If these large shapes won't fit past the metal sole, make your auxiliary sole from a 1-inch-thick piece of wood, as shown in the next photo. Glue the wood shapes low on the blade so they don't hit the metal sole on the upstroke.**

4 **Wrap sandpaper around** the leather-covered blade or wooden shape, securing it with spray adhesive. Adjust the saw speed as slow as it will go, and begin sanding. If the sanding progresses too slowly, increase the saw speed. You know you're sanding too fast if the wood begins to burn or the sandpaper loads up quickly.

Victorian Oak Mantel

In this chapter...

PRACTICAL KNOW-HOW

Routing Hardwoods and
Sheet Materials   93

Routing Raised Panels   96

Routing Turnings and
Cylinders   100

Cutting Cove
Molding   104

JIGS AND FIXTURES

Fluting Jig   99

Parallel Rule   104

SHOP SOLUTIONS

Splitting the Column   98

Repairing a
Miter Joint   106

Making a Bump-Out   107

A mantel does for a fireplace what a frame does for a picture. It directs your gaze and enhances the visual effect of a cheerful fire. And like a picture frame, it can be very simple or very ornate, depending on the visual effect you want to create. This Victorian Oak Mantel, designed and built by craftsman Larry Callahan, mimics an ornate Greek or Roman building, with fluted columns on either side supporting an intricately shaped entablature (the mantel) and architrave (the fireplace opening).

The columns, the entablature, and the moldings around the architrave make this a router project. The shape of the entablature is built up of multiple moldings, all but one of which can be made with a router. The architrave moldings are simpler, but they are also routed. Larry turned the columns, but he routed the flutes on them with the aid of a special jig that enables a router to cut turned workpieces.

What size should it be?

For the most part, the size of the mantel is determined by the size of the fireplace. Nowadays, that means the size of the *firebox,* since most new fireplaces are built around pre-assembled metal boxes. Some of these are made for wood only; some are made for gas and have ceramic logs to mimic a wood fire. Larry's fireplace swings both ways — he can lay a wood fire or light the gas. The mantel surrounds the firebox — a hearth below, columns on the sides, entablature above.

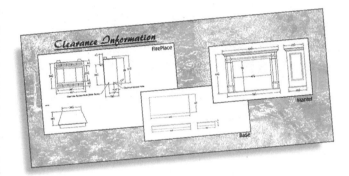

When you choose a firebox, it should come with a detailed 3-view that shows the outside dimensions. It will also specify clearances — how close you can place the flammable materials (such as wood) to the firebox. Many fireboxes today are so well insulated that they boast *zero* clearance, but it's best to check carefully.

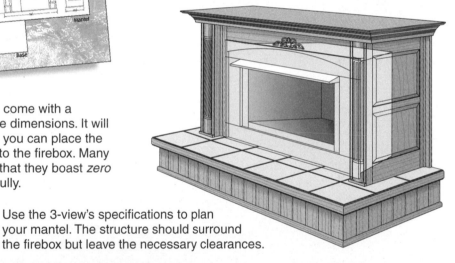

Use the 3-view's specifications to plan your mantel. The structure should surround the firebox but leave the necessary clearances.

TRY THIS!

Some fireboxes are very small, so small they would look out of place in a full-sized mantel. No problem. You can enlarge the space the firebox seems to fill by making a *firewall* — a sheet of material just behind the fireplace opening faced with tile, brick, or stone. Cut a second opening in the firewall — smaller than the mantel opening — for the firebox.

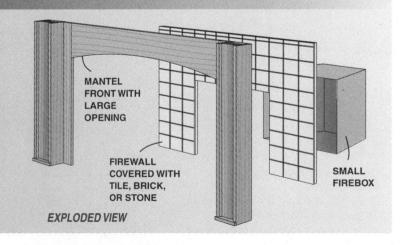

MANTEL FRONT WITH LARGE OPENING

FIREWALL COVERED WITH TILE, BRICK, OR STONE

SMALL FIREBOX

EXPLODED VIEW

CABINET OR CUTOUT?

The size of the mantel (and, to a certain extent, its construction) is also determined by how you install the firebox in your home. Traditional fireboxes require that you cut a hole in your wall and run a vent to the outside to eliminate the smoke or the gases. *Vent-free* fireboxes are much simpler to install — you can set them wherever you want them without altering the structure of your house.

If you place the firebox near a wall without cutting through it, you must make the mantel structure deep enough to cover the box. In essence, the mantel becomes a large cabinet with an opening in the front for the firebox.

Larry chose not to do this, and it wasn't just because he needed to vent the firebox. The room where he installed the firebox was relatively small, and he didn't want to give up the space that a large cabinet would have demanded. So he cut an opening in the wall for the firebox and built a "bump-out" on the outside of his home to cover it.

Larry not only built a bump-out to cover the portion of the firebox that protruded from his home, he also constructed a chimney and flue to vent the gas and smoke. This is not difficult to make, but Larry points out that it turns one project into two. The work on the outside of his home took as much time as the work inside.

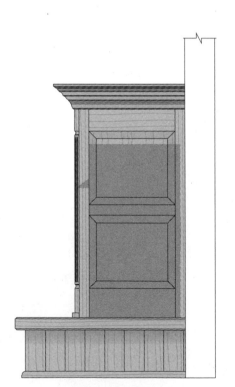

If you install the firebox inside the walls of your home, the mantel must be deep enough to cover it. If I were going to do it this way, I'd look for a fairly shallow firebox (no more than 18 inches deep). If the firebox is too deep, the mantel begins to look like an armoire on steroids.

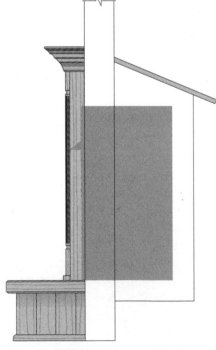

If you cut a hole in the wall for the insert, the mantel need not be quite so deep. But you must build a cover for it on the outside of your home.

What style will it be?

Larry built his mantel in a Victorian Oak style, popular around the turn of the century, when his house was built. This school of design evolved from the industrial interpretation of Victorian design. It was the first furniture style to be mass produced. Victorian Oak pieces were commonly made from white oak because it was plentiful, it machined well, and it stood up well to the rigors of shipping. In the United States, the center of the late Victorian furniture industry was in Grand Rapids, Michigan; hence the style is sometimes referred to as Grand Rapids design.

If this style doesn't work well in your home, there are other ways to go, including the two shown here:

COUNTRY STYLE

This is a "country" interpretation of architectural designs from the same Empire period. The craftsman who built this mantel at the Workshops of David T. Smith imagined himself to be an early-nineteenth-century craftsman working for clients of limited means and simple tastes. The mantel is heavy and geometric, but much of the ornamentation is painted on.

EMPIRE STYLE

In the late eighteenth century, architects and furniture makers revived the classical styles of Greece and Rome. As Napoleon established his empire in Europe, these neoclassical designs became heavier, more severe, and geometric. This mantel was crafted by Judy Ditmer — a turner of national renown — in the Empire style. It features an "overmantel" — framed mirrors and mirror-backed shelves that increase the size and ornament of the mantel.

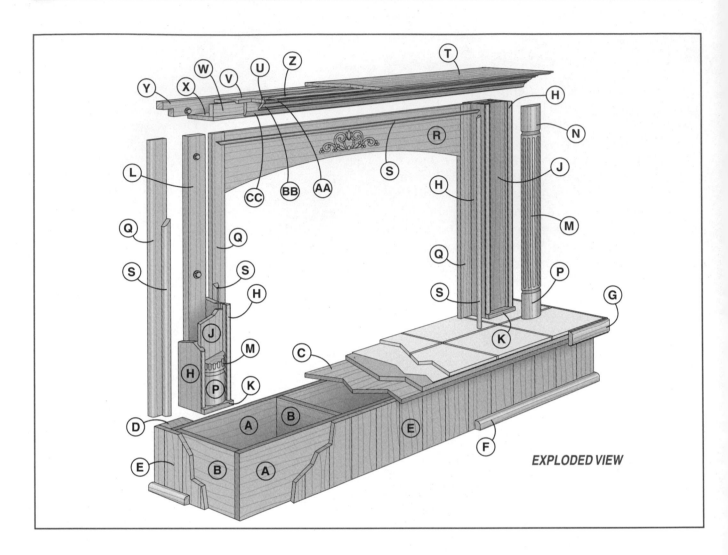

EXPLODED VIEW

VICTORIAN OAK MANTEL ■ MATERIALS LIST (Finished Dimensions)

PARTS

A	Hearth front/back (2)*	$\frac{3}{4}'' \times 10'' \times 62\frac{1}{2}''$
B	Hearth sides/dividers (5)*	$\frac{3}{4}'' \times 10'' \times 10\frac{1}{8}''$
C	Hearth top*	$\frac{3}{4}'' \times 15\frac{1}{4}'' \times 66\frac{3}{4}''$
D	Hearth cleats (2)	$1\frac{1}{2}'' \times 3\frac{1}{2}'' \times 10''$
E	Hearth facing (total)	$\frac{3}{4}'' \times 10'' \times 92''$
F	Hearth toe molding (total)	$\frac{3}{4}'' \times 1\frac{1}{4}'' \times 96''$
G	Hearth top molding (total)	$\frac{3}{4}'' \times 2\frac{1}{2}'' \times 101''$
H	Column box sides (4)	$\frac{3}{4}'' \times 3\frac{1}{4}'' \times 41\frac{3}{4}''$
J	Column box fronts (2)	$\frac{3}{4}'' \times 4\frac{1}{8}'' \times 41\frac{3}{4}''$
K	Column box bottoms (2)	$\frac{3}{4}'' \times 4\frac{7}{8}'' \times 4\frac{7}{8}''$
L	Column cleats (2)	$1\frac{1}{2}'' \times 3\frac{3}{8}'' \times 41\frac{3}{4}''$
M	Split columns (2)†	$1\frac{1}{8}'' \times 3\frac{3}{8}'' \times 30\frac{5}{8}''$
N	Split column tops (2)†	$1\frac{1}{8}'' \times 3\frac{3}{8}'' \times 5\frac{1}{8}''$
P	Split column bottoms (2)†	$1\frac{1}{8}'' \times 3\frac{3}{8}'' \times 5\frac{3}{4}''$
Q	Architrave stiles (4)	$\frac{3}{4}'' \times 1\frac{1}{2}'' \times 42\frac{1}{2}''$
R	Architrave rail	$\frac{3}{4}'' \times 10\frac{3}{4}'' \times 45''$
S	Architrave bead (total)	$\frac{3}{4}'' \times \frac{3}{4}'' \times 224''$
T	Mantel top	$\frac{3}{4}'' \times 8\frac{1}{8}'' \times 69''$
U	Upper mantel box front	$\frac{3}{4}'' \times 1\frac{1}{2}'' \times 64\frac{1}{4}''$
V	Upper mantel box bottom*	$\frac{3}{4}'' \times 3\frac{11}{16}'' \times 64\frac{1}{4}''$
W	Lower mantel box front	$\frac{3}{4}'' \times 2\frac{3}{8}'' \times 59\frac{1}{2}''$
X	Lower mantel box bottom	$\frac{3}{4}'' \times 4\frac{1}{8}'' \times 59\frac{1}{2}''$
Y	Mantel cleat	$1\frac{1}{2}'' \times 3\frac{1}{2}'' \times 64\frac{1}{2}''$
Z	Mantel top ogee molding (total)	$\frac{3}{4}'' \times 1\frac{1}{2}'' \times 84''$
AA	Mantel cove molding (total)	$\frac{1}{2}'' \times 1\frac{1}{2}'' \times 84''$
BB	Mantel crown molding (total)	$\frac{3}{4}'' \times 1\frac{15}{16}'' \times 78''$
CC	Mantel bottom ogee molding (total)	$\frac{3}{4}'' \times 2'' \times 74''$

*Make these parts from plywood.

†See page 95 for turning stock dimensions.

HARDWARE

⅜″ × 4″ Lag screws (18)

#10 × 1¼″ Flathead wood screws (40–50)

4d Finishing nails (30–40)

Appliqué

Fireplace insert or firebox

Sheet-cement substrate (8 sq. ft.)

Ceramic tile (8 sq. ft.)

Tile adhesive

Note: Larry created the effect of a firewall (see page 89) by applying tile directly to the wall of his home, around the opening he cut for the firebox. This required an extra 16 square feet of tile. If you need to build the firewall, you'll also need an extra 16 square feet of drywall or another suitable substrate.

How do I build it?

A mantel is a *built-in* project. It's attached permanently to the structure of your home, and it relies on that structure for much of its support. And like most built-in projects, it's made in three basic steps.

- First, build the basic structure.
- Then install the structure in your home.
- Finally, trim it out.

The important difference between this project and other built-ins is the third step. On most built-ins, the trim is fairly modest. On the mantel, it's the trim that makes the project.

ANOTHER WAY TO GO

Larry added the moldings to this project *after* he installed the basic structure, and on the few mantels I've helped install, that's how I did it. Jim, however, has another approach. He adds as many moldings as he can to the structure *before* it's installed, then attaches the assembly to the wall. I like to do this work on site because it allows me to fit the molding to uneven walls; Jim likes to do this sort of work in his shop because he has quick access to all his tools. Which approach is better? Whichever one works best for you.

PREPARING THE MATERIALS

For this project, you'll need both 4/4 (four-quarters) and 8/4 (eight-quarters) lumber for the mantel, columns, and hearth trim. You'll also need some plywood for the hearth and a few 2 × 4s for the cleats. Bring the wood and plywood into your shop and let it "shop dry" for a week or more before you work it. This gives the stock a chance to reach equilibrium with the relative humidity in your shop.

When the wood is ready to work, plane the 4/4 lumber down to ¾ inch thick. Plane the 8/4 stock to 1¾ inches and 1¼ inches thick to make the stock you need for the split columns.

SHOP SAVVY ■ *Routing Hardwoods and Sheet Materials*

The white oak from which Larry made his mantel is extremely hard and dense, and it is harder to rout than softer woods. So is the plywood in this project. Because the plies have opposing grains, and the glue used in plywood is slightly abrasive, it will wear down an ordinary router bit faster than other materials.

If you do a lot of routing in hard, dense woods and sheet goods, consider purchasing router bits designed especially for these materials. General-purpose router bits have *straight flutes* (1), designed for cutting both hardwoods and softwoods. Bits with *spiral flutes* (2) are also intended for hardwoods and softwoods, but the spiral design helps clear the chips when making deep cuts. *Shear flutes* (3) have angled cutting edges that leave a smoother cut and require less effort when plowing through hard, dense woods. *Stagger-tooth* (4) and *chip-breaker flutes* (5) are designed for cutting plywood and particleboard.

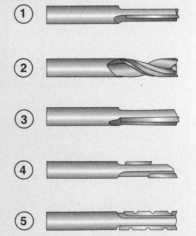

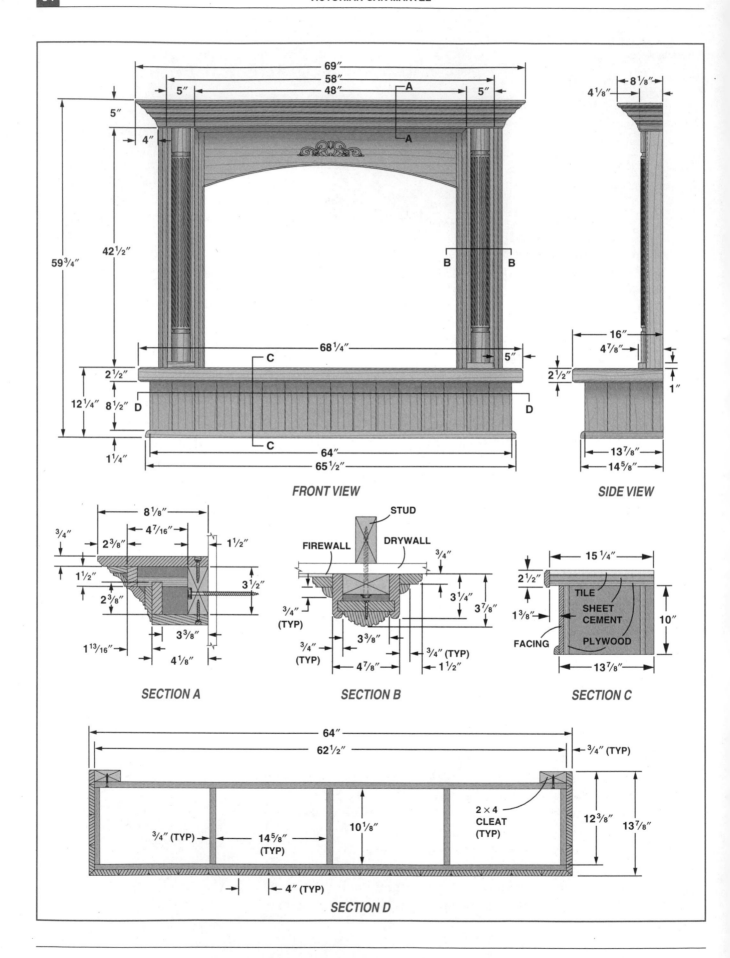

FRONT VIEW

SIDE VIEW

SECTION A

SECTION B

SECTION C

SECTION D

GLUING UP TURNING STOCK Glue the 1¼-inch and 1¾-inch-thick pieces face to face to make two turning blocks — one 31 inches long for the split columns and the other 12 inches long for the column tops and bottoms. When gluing up, insert sheets of kraft paper between the adjoining pieces; this will make it easier to split the turning later on.

MAKING THE BOXES

The mantel is built up of four simple boxes. At the bottom is the hearth box — this is the only box that's made of plywood. Just above this are two vertical assemblies, the column boxes. The mantel box rests on these.

BOX JOINERY The box joinery is as simple is it gets. With a few exceptions, the parts of the boxes are assembled with butt joints. The only joinery to speak of are some notches in the column box bottoms, as shown in the *Column Box Bottom Layout,* and a few grooves in the column boxes and mantel boxes. The column box fronts rest in ¾-inch-wide, ⅜-inch-deep grooves in the sides, as shown in *Section B.* The upper mantel front fits a groove in the mantel top, and the lower mantel front fits a groove in the upper mantel bottom, as shown in *Section A.* Rout these grooves with a straight bit.

Screw the hearth box parts together — the screws won't show when the mantel is complete. Glue the mantel fronts to the mantel bottoms; let the glue dry, then glue the mantel box assemblies to each other. *Don't* attach the mantel top yet. Dry assemble the column box fronts and sides to check the joints, but *don't* glue these together yet. Both the mantel top and the column sides require some shaping before you can glue them up.

MAKING DEEPER BOXES The drawings show a mantel that's designed to frame a firebox that's installed in a cutout in the wall. Because of this, the boxes are fairly shallow. If you don't want to cut a hole in your wall, and you want to completely cover the firebox with the mantel, you must make all five boxes deeper. Extend the sides, tops, and bottoms of the boxes as needed. You may also have to add a *firewall* to the assembly (see page 89).

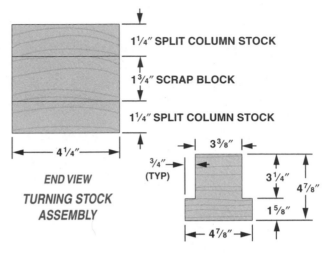

1¼" SPLIT COLUMN STOCK

1¾" SCRAP BLOCK

1¼" SPLIT COLUMN STOCK

4¼"

END VIEW
TURNING STOCK ASSEMBLY

¾" (TYP)

3⅜"

3¼"

4⅞"

1⅝"

4⅞"

COLUMN BOX BOTTOM LAYOUT

Note: You don't have to extend the *inside* sides or the bottom of the column boxes. And depending on how far you stretch the boxes, you may want to add some ribs to the mantel boxes.

SAFEGUARD

When figuring how much to extend the boxes, carefully check the information that was supplied with your firebox for any required clearances. Even some manufacturers of "zero-clearance" fireplaces recommend an inch clearance in their spec sheets.

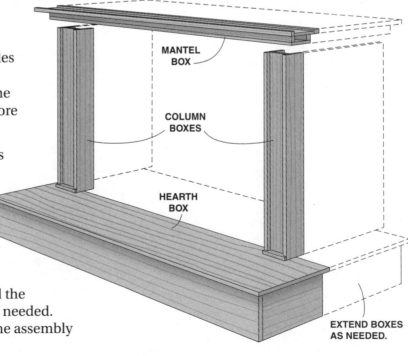

MANTEL BOX

COLUMN BOXES

HEARTH BOX

EXTEND BOXES AS NEEDED.

METHODS OF WORK ■ *Routing Raised Panels*

As I mentioned earlier, a cabinet that completely encloses a firebox may stand out from the wall a good distance. If you make the sides from solid wood or plywood, they present a large, unbroken, visually uninteresting expanse of wood. This will make the cabinet look deeper than it really is. You can break up this expanse and create some design interest by substituting a frame-and-panel assembly with raised panels.

FRAME-AND-PANEL JOINERY

You can create these assemblies with the aid of a table-mounted router. The frame consists of horizontal *rails* joined to vertical *stiles*. Both the rails and stiles have grooves in the inside edges. If you have one or more middle rails in your assembly, these have grooves in both edges. The rails have short "stub" tenons on the ends that fit the grooves. You can create both the grooves and the matching tenons on a router table with a straight bit.

> **Look Here!** For more information on routing tenons, see page 38; on routing grooves, see page 14.

The panels rest in the grooves in the rails and stiles. Because the panels are traditionally made from pieces of wood the same thickness as the rails and stiles, the panel must be thinned out at the edges to fit the grooves. The thick portion of the panel or *field* is said to be "raised."

To raise a panel with a router, use a vertical panel-raising bit. These come in several different profiles — straight bevel, cove, and ogee. Rout around the edge of each panel, forming a tongue that fits the grooves in the rails and stiles.

When assembling the frame and panel, glue the rails to the stiles, but let the panels "float" in the grooves — they must be free to expand and contract.

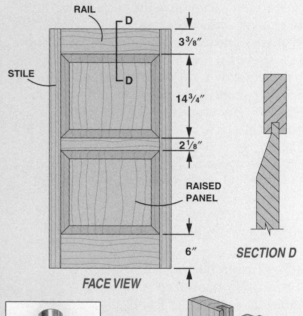

RAIL

STILE

3⅜"

14¾"

2⅛"

RAISED PANEL

6"

FACE VIEW

SECTION D

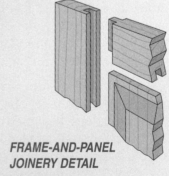

FRAME-AND-PANEL JOINERY DETAIL

Thin the edges and rout the profile of a raised panel with a *vertical panel-raising bit* (shown in the insert). Rout the ends first, then the edges. That way, if the stock chips slightly when you're cutting perpendicular to the grain, you will remove the chipped portion when you rout parallel to the grain.

TURNING THE COLUMN

To make the split columns, you must first create the shape, *then* split the shapes from the cylinder. Additionally, you must make two separate turnings to create the split columns — one for the top and bottom sections, and the other for the middle section. The reason Larry did it this way is that his lathe, like most home-shop lathes, has a capacity of only 36 inches, and the column is 42½ inches long. If you have access to a long-bed lathe, you can make the split columns with one turning.

TURNING THE SPINDLES Start with the top and bottom sections. Turn the stock round, cut the coves, and finish sand the spindle. Using a parting tool, cut partway through the spindle where you want to separate the top and bottom shapes. Remove the spindle from the lathe, and finish cutting it apart with a handsaw or on the band saw.

Next, turn a cylinder for the middle part of the column. Finish sand the surface on the lathe, but don't cut any other shapes in it. **Note: It's extremely important that you locate the lathe centers *precisely* in the center of the middle boards in the turning stock.**

ROUTING THE FLUTES If you have a lathe with an indexing head, you can easily rout the flutes in the column while the stock is still mounted on the lathe. Unfortunately lathes with indexing heads cost big bucks, so they're not all that common in a home workshop. But don't let that stop you. Instead, make a Fluting Jig (see page 99) to hold and index the cylinder while you rout the flutes.

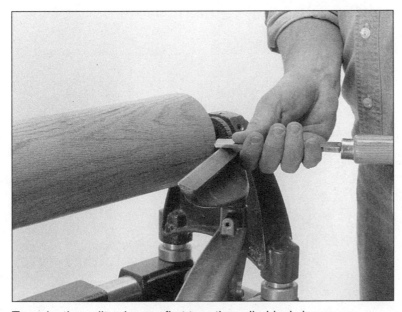

To make the split columns, first turn the cylindrical shapes on a lathe.

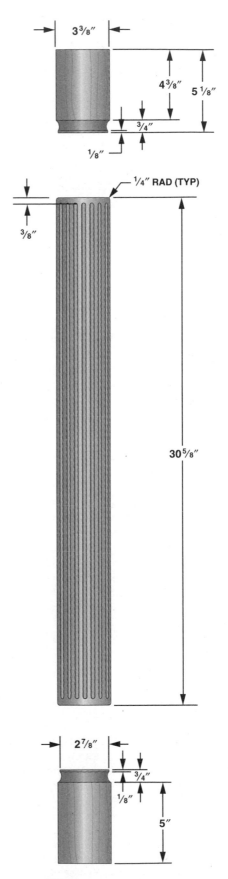

3⅜″
4⅜″   5⅛″
¾″
⅛″

¼″ RAD (TYP)
⅜″

30⅝″

2⅞″
¾″
⅛″
5″

VERTICAL COLUMN LAYOUT

By the way, even though the fixture is called a fluting jig, you can rout beads, flats, ogees, and other shapes with it, as well as cut mortises and grooves in round stock.

SPLITTING THE COLUMN After routing the flutes, place the cutting edge of a chisel along one of the glue-and-paper joints between the boards in the spindle turnings. Whack it firmly with a mallet, and the stock will separate at the joint. Repeat for all the shapes — top, bottom, and middle — and all the seams to make two copies of each shape.

Wet down the paper on the back of the split turnings and let it sit for a few minutes to partially dissolve the glue. Then scrape the glue and paper away with a hand scraper or shave hook.

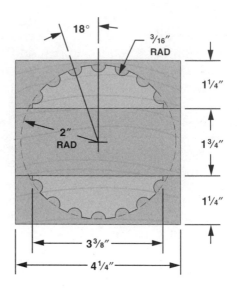

SPLIT COLUMN FLUTE LAYOUT

Rout the stopped flutes in the middle column with the stock mounted in a Fluting Jig. This guides the router and indexes the turning so the flutes are evenly spaced. Note that you don't have to rout flutes all around the turning, just in those portions that will become the split columns.

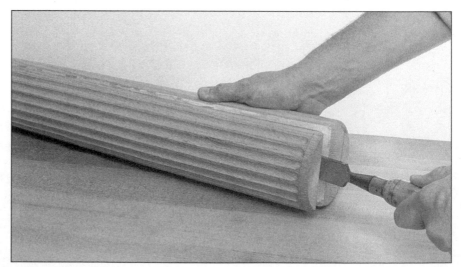

Split off the portions of the turnings that you need for the split columns by driving a chisel into the paper seam between the boards. Once started, the pieces will separate cleanly and easily. The fibers in the paper aren't as strong as those in the wood, so they split without breaking the wood. **Note: This technique only works with a heavyweight paper, such as kraft paper. Newspaper is too light and thin.**

QUICK FIXTURE ■ *Fluting Jig*

A fluting jig performs the following three functions:

■ It holds a spindle turning or cylindrical stock while you rout the surface.

■ It supports and guides the router.

■ It indexes the turning, allowing you to rotate it a specific number of degrees between each cut.

Make the fluting jig shown from ¾-inch-thick plywood. The distance between the inside surfaces of the supports should be equal to the length of the turning *plus* the thickness of the indexing wheel. The height of the supports is determined by the diameter of the turning.

Bevel the inside edges of the platform parts so they won't interfere with the turning. If the jig is extremely long and the platform sags under the weight of the router, brace each part with a strip of wood glued edge-to-face against the bottom face of the platform part.

Using a protractor, lay out the indexing wheel, drawing evenly spaced lines on one face. Cut the wheel the same diameter as — or just ⅛ to ¼ inch larger than — the turning. Using a small square, transfer the lines to the edge of the wheel. Also make an alignment mark on the jig, centered between the platform parts.

Drill holes in the supports for pivot screws and a locking screw (to keep the stock from rotating). Center each hole below the opening in the platform. To figure the distance of each pivot hole from the top edge of its support, subtract ¼ to ½ inch from the radius of the turning. Place the center of the indexing wheel over the mark for each pivot hole to check that the turning won't hit the platform.

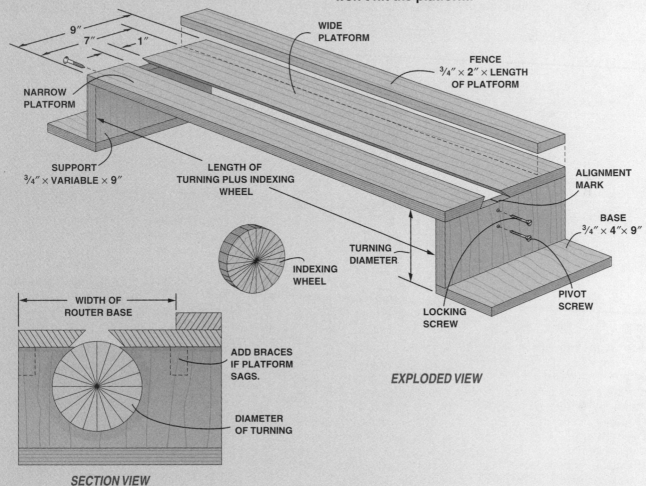

EXPLODED VIEW

SECTION VIEW

SHOP SAVVY   *Routing Turnings and Cylinders*

Using a router in conjunction with a lathe opens up a whole range of design possibilities. Lathe tools cut perpendicular to the axis of the turning, but the router lets you cut parallel to the axis as well. This, in turn, lets you cut flutes, reeds, and similar shapes in a turning. A lathe turning, however, is a cylinder; and in order to rout it, you must build a special jig to hold the turning and guide the router. (See page 99.)

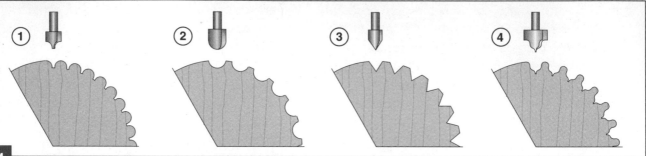

1   **Decide what shape** you want to create in the turning and what bit you will use to make it. To rout traditional reeds (or beads) in a spindle, use an unpiloted roundover bit or *beading bit* (1). For traditional flutes, use a *roundnose bit* (2). You can also use other unpiloted point-cut and top-cut router bits to create nontraditional shapes. A *V-groove bit* (3), for example, cuts a V-shaped flute. An unpiloted *ogee bit* (4) makes a combination reed and flute.

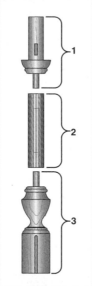

2   **Consider where you're going** to rout the shapes on the turning. Depending on the profile of the spindle, you may have to divide the turning into two or more parts to rout it. On this tip-and-turn table, for example, the routed portion of the spindle (with the vertical reeds) is smaller in diameter than most of the other turned shapes. The larger shapes would have gotten in the way during the routing operation, so Larry made the spindle in three sections. The middle section was a simple cylinder in which he routed the reeds.

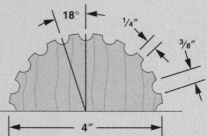

3   **Figure the spacing,** in degrees, between each cut as you rout the spindle. Make a test cut in a scrap and measure the width of the cut. If you're routing reeds, the width will be equal to the cutting diameter of the beading bit. If you're cutting flutes, the spacing will be equal to the diameter of the roundnose bit *plus* the width of the area you want to leave between each flute. Calculate the circumference of the turning by multiplying the diameter by π (3.1416), then divide the circumference by the width of cut. (If you come up with a fraction, round *down* to the nearest whole number.) Divide this number into 360 — the number of degrees in a full circle — to find the angular spacing between each cut. In the 4-inch-diameter columns in the mantle, for example, the flutes are ⅜ inch wide and there is ¼ inch between each flute:

$$(4 \times 3.1416) \div (\tfrac{3}{8} + \tfrac{1}{4}) = 20.1062$$

This rounds down to 20. If we were to cut 20 flutes, evenly spaced around the spindle, they would have to be 18 degrees apart:

$$360 \div 20 = 18$$

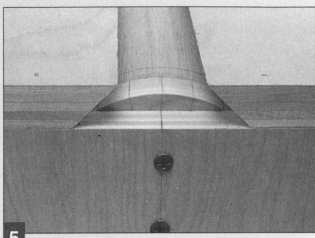

4 **Make an indexing wheel** (see page 99), then fasten the wheel to one end of the turning with two wood screws, carefully aligning the center of the wheel with the turning axis. Mount the turning in a *Fluting Jig* (see page 99) by driving roundhead wood screws through the ends of the jig and into the ends of the turning at the axis. The turning and the wheel must rotate together on the screws.

5 **Align one of the marks** on the indexing wheel with the alignment mark on the fluting jig. Drive the locking screw through the support and into the indexing wheel and the turning. This will prevent the turning from moving as you rout.

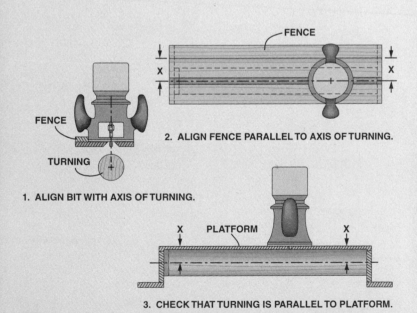

FENCE

FENCE

X   X

2. ALIGN FENCE PARALLEL TO AXIS OF TURNING.

FENCE

TURNING

1. ALIGN BIT WITH AXIS OF TURNING.

X   PLATFORM   X

3. CHECK THAT TURNING IS PARALLEL TO PLATFORM.

6 **Position the fence** on the fluting jig, and clamp it in place. The fence must be parallel to the axis or centerline of the turning. Additionally, when the router base is against the fence, the axis of the bit should be directly over the axis of the turning. Also check that the turning is parallel to the jig platform. Adjust the depth of cut so the tip of the router bit just touches the turning, and guide the router along the fence *without* turning it on. The bit should remain in contact with the area you wish to rout.

7 Adjust the depth of cut to rout the shape in the turning. Turn the router on and make the first cut, guiding the router along the fence. Turn the router off, remove the locking screw, and rotate the turning and indexing wheel until the next mark on the wheel aligns with the indicator mark on the jig. Secure the turning with the locking screw, and make another cut. Continue until you have made all the cuts that you need. On most turnings, you must cut all the way around the cylinder. On the split turning for the mantel, you can skip a few flutes, as shown in the *Split Column Flute Layout* on page 98.

SHAPING THE MOLDINGS AND EDGES

There are six moldings to make for this project. Additionally, there are a number of shaped edges to rout.

SIMPLE SHAPES Begin with the moldings and edges that need only a single pass. Rout:

- One edge and both ends of the *mantel top,* using a *cove-and-bead bit*
- Sufficient stock for the *mantel top ogee molding* using a ½-inch ogee bit
- Sufficient stock for the *mantel bottom ogee molding,* using a vertical *ogee panel-raising bit*
- Sufficient stock for the *hearth toe molding* and the *architrave bead molding,* using a ½-inch roundover bit
- One edge of the *outside architrave stiles,* using a ¼-inch roundover bit

COMPLEX SHAPES Next, make the moldings that require multiple passes. Rout:

- Both arrises of the outside edges of the *column box sides* and both edges of the *hearth top molding,* using a ¼-inch roundover bit
- The face of the *mantel crown molding* using a *crown molding bit,* and the *back arrises* using a *chamfer bit*

Note: You can substitute other shapes for those shown, if desired.

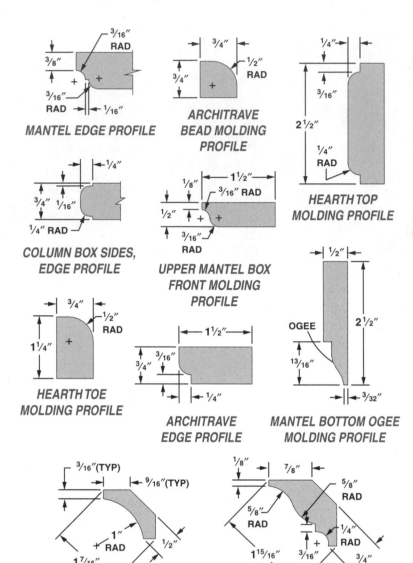

MANTEL EDGE PROFILE

ARCHITRAVE BEAD MOLDING PROFILE

HEARTH TOP MOLDING PROFILE

COLUMN BOX SIDES, EDGE PROFILE

UPPER MANTEL BOX FRONT MOLDING PROFILE

HEARTH TOE MOLDING PROFILE

ARCHITRAVE EDGE PROFILE

MANTEL BOTTOM OGEE MOLDING PROFILE

MANTEL COVE MOLDING PROFILE

MANTEL CROWN MOLDING PROFILE

The mantel crown molding is a *sprung* molding; that is, it's installed at an angle. Because of this, the back arrises must be cut on a diagonal. Cut the front face with a vertical crown molding bit *(left),* then bevel the back arrises with a chamfer bit *(right).*

COVE MOLDING While the chamfer bit is mounted in the router, bevel all four arrises of the cove molding stock. You could cut the face with a vertical cove molding bit, similar to the crown molding bit. But these bits are expensive, and there's no sense in investing in one for this one project as long as you have a table saw. Cut the cove in the face of the molding by passing the stock over the saw blade at an angle. (See page 104.)

INSTALLING THE BOXES

Finish sand the shaped profiles, and attach the mantel top to the mantel box with glue. Also glue together the column box sides and fronts. Screw the column box bottoms and the split columns to the fronts. Drive the screws that hold the columns from the *inside* of the boxes so they won't show on the completed mantel.

INSTALLING THE HEARTH Attach the hearth cleats to the wall, and screw the hearth box to the cleats. Secure the cleats to the wall with lag screws, or if this isn't possible, use expandable "molly" anchors.

Attach the plywood top to the hearth, then cover that with a sheet-cement product (such as Durock). Install the sheet cement with a mastic adhesive (such as Liquid Nails). Apply tile to the sheet cement using a tile adhesive. Don't grout between the tile just yet.

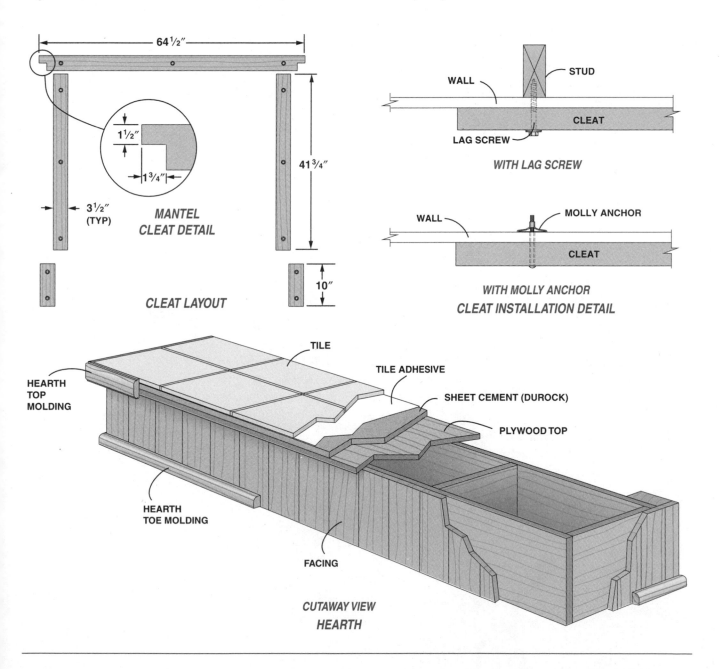

64½"

1½"

1¾"

3½"
(TYP)

**MANTEL
CLEAT DETAIL**

41¾"

10"

CLEAT LAYOUT

WALL

STUD

CLEAT

LAG SCREW

WITH LAG SCREW

WALL

MOLLY ANCHOR

CLEAT

WITH MOLLY ANCHOR
CLEAT INSTALLATION DETAIL

TILE

TILE ADHESIVE

SHEET CEMENT (DUROCK)

PLYWOOD TOP

HEARTH
TOP
MOLDING

HEARTH
TOE MOLDING

FACING

CUTAWAY VIEW
HEARTH

SHOP SAVVY ■ *Cutting Cove Molding*

To cut a cove with a larger radius than is commonly available in a router bit, use a table saw. Pass the molding stock over a *combination blade,* guiding it along a straightedge at an angle to the blade. The width of the cove is determined by the angle and position of the straightedge; the depth is determined by the height of the blade at the last pass.

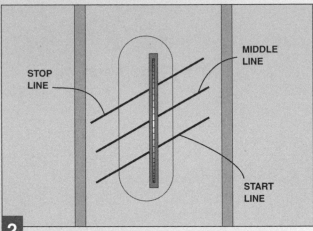

1   **To find the coving angle** — the angle at which the work must cross the blade — use a simple shop-made *parallel rule.* Adjust the blade to the desired depth of cut, and set the rule to the desired width of the cove. Place the rule on the saw table, straddling the blade. Turn it at various angles to the blade while rotating the blade by hand. Find the position where the teeth of the saw brush both the front and back rules. Using a grease pencil, trace the *inside edge* of each rule, making two parallel lines on the table.

2   **Measure the distance** between the front and back lines, then draw a third line halfway between the two and parallel to them. This marks the center of the cove cut. Use all three lines as references to determine the angle and position of the straightedge that guides the work. For example, if you want to cut a cove down the center of a 2-inch-wide board, the straightedge must be parallel to and 1 inch away from the middle reference line. Fasten the straightedge to the table with clamps or double-faced carpet tape.

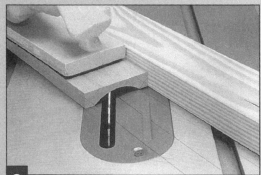

3   **Adjust the saw blade** so it protrudes about 1/16 inch above the table. Turn on the saw and place the work against the straight-edge. Slowly feed the work from the infeed side of the saw, against the rotation of the blade. After completing the first pass, raise the saw blade another 1/16 inch and make another cut. Repeat until you have cut the cove to the desired depth. Sand the coved surface smooth.

QUICK FIXTURE ■ *Parallel Rule*

Make a parallel rule from four strips of wood. Fasten the strips together at the corners with roundhead wood screws. Don't overtighten the screws — the joined rules should pivot easily.

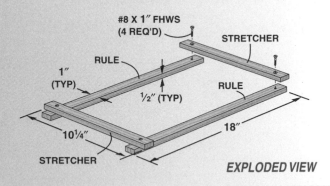

EXPLODED VIEW

Installing the Columns. Attach the column cleats to the wall, then screw the columns to the cleats. (The heads of these screws will later be covered by vertical stiles.) The column box bottoms should rest on the tile-covered hearth.

Installing the Mantel. Attach the mantel cleat to the wall above the columns. Because this cleat supports a heavy assembly, make sure it's secured to the studs in the wall in at least two locations. Attach the mantel box to the cleat with screws. When installed, the mantel should rest on the column boxes.

INSTALLING THE FIREWALL AND ENTABLATURE

Measure the distance between the column boxes. If the distance is different from what you figured when you planned this project, adjust the length of the entablature rail to compensate. Assemble the rails and stiles, using biscuits, splines, or dowels, whichever you prefer. Let the glue dry, then shape the inside edges of the architrave with a ¼-inch roundover bit, as shown in the *Architrave Edge Profile* on page 102.

If your design includes a firewall, attach 1-inch-square cleats to the inside sides of the column boxes with glue and screws. These cleats should run vertically the entire length of the column boxes. Attach the firewall to the cleats with drywall screws. If you have elected to do so, apply tile to the wall or the firewall, using tile adhesive. Secure the architrave to the column boxes and the tiled wall (or firewall) with mastic adhesive.

APPLYING THE DECORATIVE ELEMENTS

Once installed, the boxes complete the structure of the mantel. But you'll need to install the moldings and the other decorative elements to make it look like a mantel.

COVERING THE HEARTH Choose a decorative covering for the hearth box. Larry used wainscoting, but there are many other choices, including a faux brick or stone facade. Cover the hearth cleats, sides, and front.

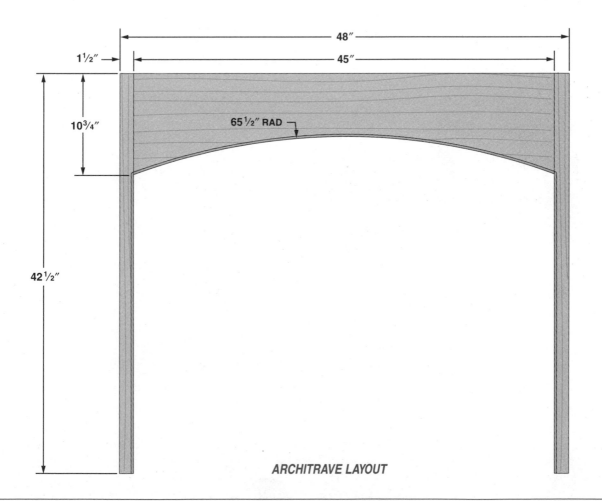

ARCHITRAVE LAYOUT

APPLYING THE MOLDINGS Working your way up, install the

- Hearth toe molding
- Hearth top molding
- Outside architrave stiles
- Architrave bead molding

When you get to the mantel, you must work your way up *and* down, installing the

- Mantel bottom ogee molding
- Mantel top ogee molding
- Mantel cove molding
- Mantel crown molding

Miter the adjoining ends of the moldings where they turn a corner. Attach the outside architrave stiles with mastic (as you did the entablature), but install the remaining parts with finish nails. Set the heads of the nails below the wood surface with a nail set. Larry covered the heads of his nails with water putty. This takes a stain better than anything Jim and I have tested so far, and it's easy to work with.

INSTALLING THE GROUT AND APPLIQUÉ After you install the hearth top molding, but before you move on to the stiles and bead molding, apply grout between the tiles on both the hearth and the wall (or firewall). Larry recommends a dark grout, especially if you intend to burn wood in your insert. Light grout is much more difficult to keep clean.

After you apply all the moldings, glue the appliqué to the entablature rail, centered between the stiles.

FINISHING THE MANTEL

The finish that you apply to the mantel will, of course, depend on the other moldings and trim in your home and your own preferences. However, before you choose a finish, think it through. In particular, consider the handwork it requires. How much sanding between coats will you have to do? How much time will you spend rubbing it out? Because of all the molded profiles on this project, a finish that requires a lot of sanding and rubbing could be more effort than it's worth.

I'm slowly restoring an old Victorian home with a lot of ornate moldings, and I've experimented

RESOURCES

You can purchase precut, premolded wooden appliqués from several mail-order woodworking suppliers, including:

The Woodworkers' Store
4365 Willow Drive
Medina, MN 55340

NO PROBLEM ■ *Repairing a Miter Joint*

You do your best to measure, but when you assemble the miter joint, one member protrudes slightly past the other. No problem, so long as you resist the easy fix. Don't sand down the end of the protruding portion — this will expose end grain at the seam. And the whole point of a miter joint is to hide the end grain. Instead, you must do a little hand shaping.

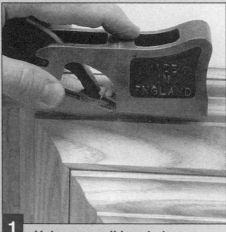

1 **Using a small hand plane,** carving chisel, or scrapes, pare down the face of the protruding member. Carefully follow the contours of the molded profile as you do this.

2 **Remove stock** from a long enough section of the work so the molded surface still looks straight to a casual observer. Stop removing wood when both members meet at the miter and neither protrudes past the other.

with a number of finishes. Here's one that produces excellent results with very little handwork.

Wipe the wood with a wet rag to raise the grain, then sand it smooth. Stain the new installation to match the existing moldings with a water-based aniline dye. (These can be easily mixed to create any color you need, and they produce vivid, permanent colors.) Blend a wipe-on tung oil finish with spar varnish, adding 2 tablespoons of varnish per cup of oil. Wipe the first coat of the mixture onto the wood with a rag or a foam brush. For subsequent coats, apply it with a fiberglass abrasive pad (such as Scotch-Brite). This levels the preceding coat and applies a new one in one step. If you want a high-gloss finish, apply the last coat with a foam brush, spreading out each brushful *as thin as possible.* Don't sand the final coat when it dries.

ALTERNATIVES ■ *Making a Bump-Out*

If you have elected to install your firebox in a cutout in the wall, as Larry did, you must do a little carpentry to frame in the cutout and create a *bump-out* on the outside of your house.

Remove the drywall or plaster from the area where you plan to install the mantel. Carefully measure where you want to make the cutout — remember, the firebox will sit slightly above the floor so the bottom edge is even with the top surface of the hearth. If necessary, cut through the wall studs where you will make the cutout and remove the sections that will be in the way. Install a 2 × 4 *sill plate* to frame the bottom edge of the cutout, a header made of two 2 × 8s nailed together to frame the top, and 2 × 4 cripples at the sides. *Don't cut through the outside wall just yet.*

Build a frame for the bump-out from 2 × 4s. The inside dimension of the frame, where it attaches to the wall, must match the outside dimensions of the cutout. On a good morning, when you're sure the weather will hold for the day, cut through the outside wall. Pare back the siding on the outside of the house to accommodate the outside dimensions of the bump-out frame.

Attach the bump-out frame to the header, cripples, and sill plate with lag screws. Then cover the frame with insulating foam, sheathing, plywood, siding, and roofing materials to match the outside of your home. Finish the inside of the bump-out with fire-resistant drywall.

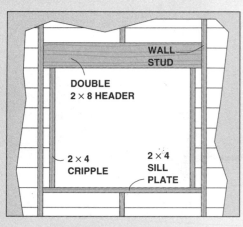

BUMP-OUT FRAMING

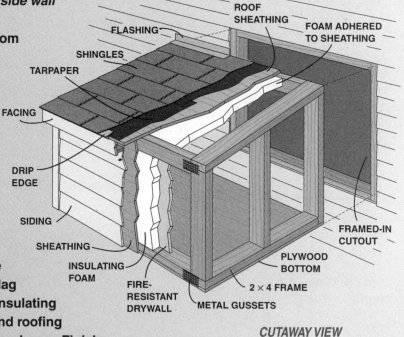

CUTAWAY VIEW

Personalized Router Table

Super-strong, dead-flat torsion-box work surface

Miter gauge slot

Mounting plate adjusts perfectly flush with work surface

Guarded starter pin lets you use piloted bits safely

Cavernous storage cabinet

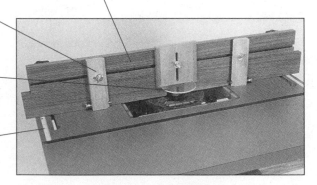

Built-in dust collector

Split fence provides maximum support and guidance

Micro-adjustable fence stops

Cutter guard doubles as depth-of-cut gauge

Centering scales to position fence accurately

Bonus Jig Features

An easy-to-make router table with "options" to adapt it to your personal woodworking needs, including:

Torsion-Box Work Surface	110
Mounting Plate	111
Depth-of-Cut Adjusters	113
Router Table Fence	114
Dust Collection	114
Fence Stops	116
Starter Pin and Guard	116
Guard and Depth Gauge	117
Fence-Positioning Scales	117
Tilt-Top Stand	118
Storage Cabinet	120

Do you roll your eyes when you see yet another woodworking book or magazine touting the "ultimate" router table? Well, you couldn't be any more tired of this hype than I am. Over the last few decades, Jim and I have been responsible for about a dozen of those fixtures, each one more ultimate than the last. And what you find as soon as you have a little experience with table-mounted routing operations is that there is no such thing as an ultimate router table, for the same reason that there's no ultimate router.

Router tables, like any complex tool, have various features and components. Depending on the kinds of woodworking you do, some of these components work for you; others may be useless or even get in your way. That being so, Jim and I have come up with a unique approach to router table design — a table that can be customized to fit your own *individual* needs.

In its simplest form it's just a work surface on a stand. The work surface may be nothing more than a thick sheet of particleboard or MDF (medium-density fiberboard); the stand is just a few butt-jointed boards that can be screwed together in an afternoon.

Beyond that, there are some exciting possibilities for you to consider. A *torsion-box* work surface is stronger and more apt to remain flat than a solid slab. A *split fence,* with built-in *dust collection* and adjustable *stops,* increases the accuracy of your work exponentially. *Keyhole slots* in the top allow

you to mount or dismount a fence in seconds. A *tilt-top stand* provides easy access to your router. A *height-adjusting mechanism* lets you change the depth of cut effortlessly. Scales attached to the cutter guard and table help set the depth of cut and fence position. A rock-solid guarded *starter pin* lets you safely use piloted bits to cut curved profiles. A storage cabinet beneath the work surface not only keeps your router accessories at the ready, it also adds weight and stability to the fixture.

Pick and choose among these features to create a "personalized" router table. Or, start with a simple table, then add features one at a time as your woodworking needs increase. This approach not only lets you tailor a router table to the woodworking you do now, but it can also evolve as you gain experience and as your interests change. If I were writing the advertising copy for this book, I might say that this really is the ultimate router table. But we all know better.

Work surface tilts for easy access to the router

Height adjuster changes depth of cut effortlessly

Keyhole slots to mount and dismount fence quickly

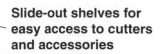

Slide-out shelves for easy access to cutters and accessories

TORSION-BOX WORK SURFACE

The most stubborn problem that plagues shop-made router tables is a work surface that's not flat. The flattest tabletop materials available to woodworkers — particleboard and MDF— are also the least strong. A heavy router, hanging from a single ¾-inch thickness of particleboard or MDF, will eventually cause the top to bow, playing havoc with the accuracy of your routing operations.

You can strengthen a table by laminating two sheets of material together or by using thick sheets — 1-inch and thicker sheet materials are available on special order from most suppliers of cabinetmaking materials. Or, you can brace the sheet materials by attaching them to a wooden grid.

ASSEMBLING A TORSION-BOX WORK SURFACE

The best approach that I've found borrows a little from both techniques. Laminate two sheets of particleboard or MDF to braces (or "ribs") *of the same material* to make a *torsion box*. The sheet materials become the top and bottom (or "skin") of the box.

Ordinarily, torsion boxes are built by simply gluing the skin to the top and bottom edges of the ribs. But I recommend you cut grooves for the braces in the skin. This lets you use more substantial ribs, creating a stronger box without increasing the overall thickness of the assembly. Glue the ribs in the grooves when you assemble the box. Also glue an additional strip of material under the area where you will rout a miter gauge groove — this reinforces the skin.

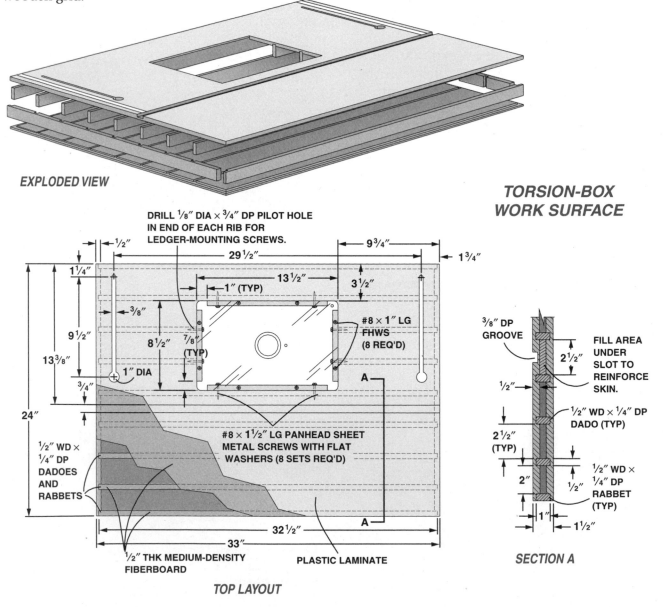

EXPLODED VIEW

TORSION-BOX
WORK SURFACE

DRILL ⅛″ DIA × ¾″ DP PILOT HOLE
IN END OF EACH RIB FOR
LEDGER-MOUNTING SCREWS.

#8 × 1″ LG FHWS (8 REQ'D)

#8 × 1½″ LG PANHEAD SHEET METAL SCREWS WITH FLAT WASHERS (8 SETS REQ'D)

½″ WD × ¼″ DP DADOES AND RABBETS

½″ THK MEDIUM-DENSITY FIBERBOARD

PLASTIC LAMINATE

TOP LAYOUT

⅜″ DP GROOVE

FILL AREA UNDER SLOT TO REINFORCE SKIN.

½″ WD × ¼″ DP DADO (TYP)

½″ WD × ¼″ DP RABBET (TYP)

SECTION A

LAMINATING THE SURFACE In addition to being weak, particleboard and MDF are also relatively soft. Because of this, the table surface will wear quickly. To sidestep this problem, cover the work surface and the edges with plastic laminate. Laminate not only creates a hard surface, it also reduces friction, giving you better control.

However, if you laminate the torsion box, cover *both* the top and bottom skin. An uncovered surface absorbs moisture more readily than a covered area. This would cause the bottom skin to expand and contract at a different rate than the top skin, and the box would warp.

INSTALLING THE MOUNTING PLATE Most woodworkers mount their router to a thin metal or plastic *mounting plate,* then install the plate in a work surface. If you attach the router directly to a work surface, the depth of cut is reduced by the thickness of the work surface. A thin plate minimizes this loss of capacity.

What sort of material should you use? I prefer $3/8$-inch-thick clear acrylic plastic because it lets me see what's happening under the table. Thinner acrylic won't adequately support a heavy router. Avoid polycarbonate plastics (such as Lexan) — these are too flexible.

How do you install the mounting plate flush with the work surface? I cut the opening with a pattern-routing bit. This lets me use the plate itself as a template to rout the recess.

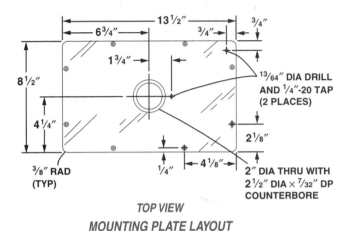

TOP VIEW
MOUNTING PLATE LAYOUT

Using a few tiny pieces of double-faced carpet tape, *lightly* stick the plate to the work surface where you want to install it. Cut strips of wood about $1/8$ inch wider than the length of the cutting flutes on the pattern-cutting bit. Build a frame around the plate, adhering the frame members *securely* to the work surface with carpet tape.

Tip: Depending on the thickness of the work surface, you may need to split each frame member into two or more pieces, then remove them one at a time as you work your way down. On the router table shown, Jim split the frame into three $1/2$-inch-thick pieces.

Attach the router to a large base, such as the base from the Router Planing Jig on page 10. With a $3/4$-inch pattern-routing bit, rout around the inside of the frame, cutting $1/8$ to $1/4$ inch deeper with each pass until you have cut completely through the work surface. On our design, the plate corners are radiused to match the rounded corners that the bit cuts. If you leave the corners of the plate square, you'll have to square the corners of the cutout.

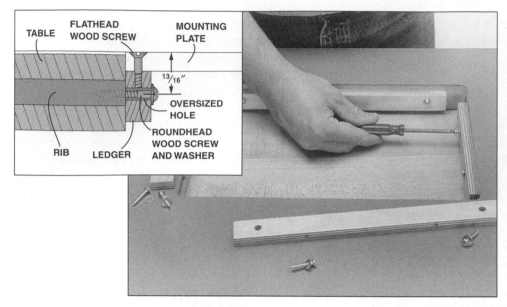

If need be, fill the voids between the ribs inside the cutout with spacers. (By carefully planning the spacing of the ribs in the top, you can make this unnecessary.) Attach ledgers to the inside edges of the cutouts, driving panhead screws through the slots in the ledgers and into the ribs or spacers. The top surface of each ledger should rest well below the work surface to accommodate the mounting plate. If the mounting plate is ⅜ inch thick, the ledgers should be approximately ⅜ inch below the top of the work surface.

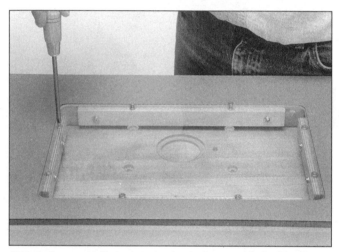

Attach the mounting plate to the ledgers with flathead wood screws. Countersink the screws so the heads rest slightly below the top surface of the plate.

The mounting holes in the ledgers are oversized to let you adjust their height a fraction of an inch. When the mounting plate is attached, loosen the panhead screws and move the ledgers up or down until the plate is flush with the work surface. Then tighten the screws.

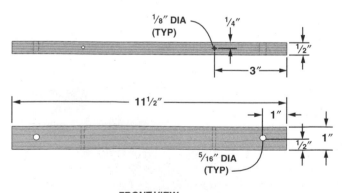

FRONT VIEW
LONG LEDGER DETAIL

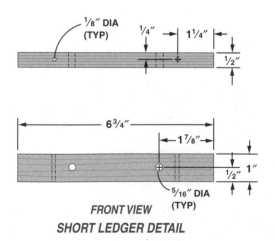

FRONT VIEW
SHORT LEDGER DETAIL

DEPTH-OF-CUT ADJUSTERS

Anyone who has ever lost their religion trying to adjust the depth of cut of a router while it's mounted under a table will appreciate these gizmos. They help set the height of the bit quickly and accurately. Depth-of-cut adjusters aren't really a component of the router table, but they are a welcome addition to any table-routing system.

FOR THE PLUNGE ROUTER The crank is designed to fit over the threaded post on a plunge router. Drill a hole in the end of the shaft just slightly larger in diameter than the post and 3 to 4 inches deep. Imbed a hex nut (the same size as the post) in the very end of the shaft, and secure it with epoxy. Remove the stop nuts from the post, and replace them with the crank. To adjust the depth of cut, loosen the depth lock and turn the crank.

There's an accessory on the market very much like this jig, I know. But it has a simple knob at the top and takes a lot of wrist action to raise or lower the router. You'll find that this adjuster's crank action is faster and more comfortable to use.

FOR THE STANDARD ROUTER If you have a standard router, make the "router jack." This is a miniature screw jack for your router. Rest it on a shelf under your table-mounted router, and turn the wheel until it contacts the router housing. Loosen the depth lock and turn the wheel. Note that I've specified a $\frac{3}{8}$-16 carriage bolt in the jack. Because there are 16 threads per inch (TPI), one turn of the wheel will raise or lower the router $\frac{1}{16}$ inch.

TRY THIS!

Replace the threaded post on your plunge router with a $\frac{3}{8}$-16 threaded post, and use a matching nut in the adjuster crank. Because these have 16 threads per inch, a single turn will raise or lower the router precisely $\frac{1}{16}$ inch; a half turn, $\frac{1}{32}$ inch; a quarter turn, $\frac{1}{64}$ inch; and so on. This is a fairly straightforward task if you're a reasonably competent machinist. If not, take your router to a machine shop and have them do it for you.

QUICK FIXTURES ■ *Router Crank and Router Jack*

FOR THE PLUNGE ROUTER

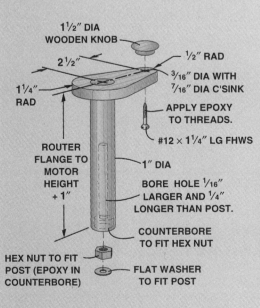

To imbed the nut, first drill a counterbore. The diameter of the counterbore should be equal to the distance from flat to flat on the nut. With a chisel, cut the counterbore to a hexagonal shape to fit the nut.

EXPLODED VIEW
Router Crank

FOR THE STANDARD ROUTER

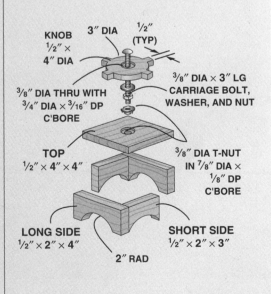

EXPLODED VIEW
Router Jack

ROUTER TABLE FENCE

Next to the work surface, the most important part of a table routing system is the fence. A good fence not only positions and guides the work but also allows you to start and stop a cut precisely. It reduces the risk of injury during router operations by allowing you to "bury" the unused portion of the bit behind the fence face, out of harm's way. And it makes a dirty job much cleaner by allowing you to collect sawdust as you rout. It's no wonder that Jim and I typically spend as much time designing and making a router table fence as we do the rest of the system. That isn't to say that a fence has to be complex.

MAKING A SIMPLE FENCE For many years, I used a simple fence made from a single board and did some dynamite woodworking with it. Just joint a thick piece of hardwood straight and true, then make a cutout in one edge for the router bits. If you wish, attach a box to the back to serve as a dust collector port (see *Dust Hookup,* below left).

MAKING A SPLIT FENCE Later on, I came to appreciate the capabilities of a *split* fence. On this design, the faces slide right and left. You can "close up" the opening around the bit, making it as small as possible. This has two advantages. First, it provides more support and better guidance for the work, reducing the risk of uneven cuts and tearout. Second, it increases the efficiency of your dust collector.

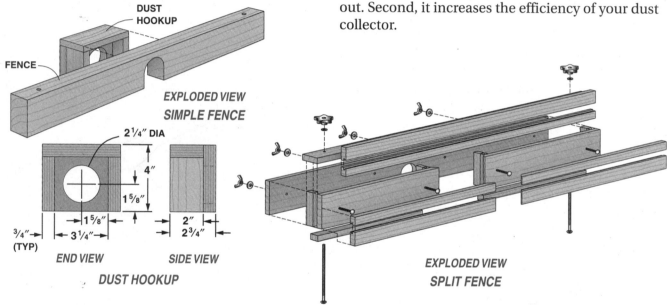

DUST HOOKUP

FENCE

EXPLODED VIEW
SIMPLE FENCE

2¼" DIA

4"

1⅝"

1⅝"

¾"
(TYP)

3¼"

END VIEW

2"

2¾"

SIDE VIEW

DUST HOOKUP

EXPLODED VIEW
SPLIT FENCE

A good split fence allows you to move the faces in and out as well as side to side. On this fence, insert a shim or a spacer between the fence bracket and the face to advance the face. Make the shims from a thin material, such as plastic laminate.

Why is this useful? Good question. During any routing operation in which you must cut the entire guiding surface of the board, you must advance the outfeed fence face in front of the infeed face. This makes up for the stock you cut away and keeps the work traveling in a straight line. **And by the way: This same setup lets you use a router for edge jointing, as shown on page 35.**

The split fence is a simple box, open on the bottom, with the fence faces secured to one side. The upper face is *fixed* — glued permanently in place on the box. The lower faces slide over the carriage bolt heads, which go all the way through the fence. Loosen the wing nuts that secure the carriage bolts, and you can slide the fence face back and forth.

All the faces — fixed and sliding — have T-slots. The T-slots on the sliding faces fit over the carriage bolts. The long slot on the fixed face allows you to mount stops, featherboards, and guards. To make the T-slots, rip the face stock in two parts. Cut a groove in the cut edges — the width of this groove should be slightly more than the thickness of the head of the carriage bolts. Then cut $5/32$ inch from

the lip on the back side of the groove, and glue the parts back together, as shown in the *Fence Detail.*

MOUNTING THE FENCE Whichever fence you decide to make, they both mount in "keyhole" slots in the work surface, as shown in the *Top Layout* on page 110. These slots have large holes at one end to slip the heads of the mounting bolts in and out. This lets you mount and dismount the fence without taking the hardware apart. To make a keyhole slot, first drill the large hole at the end of the slot. Then rout the slot completely through the work surface, ribs and all. Don't worry if the slot passes through the voids between the top and bottom skin; this won't affect the fence or the mounting bolts.

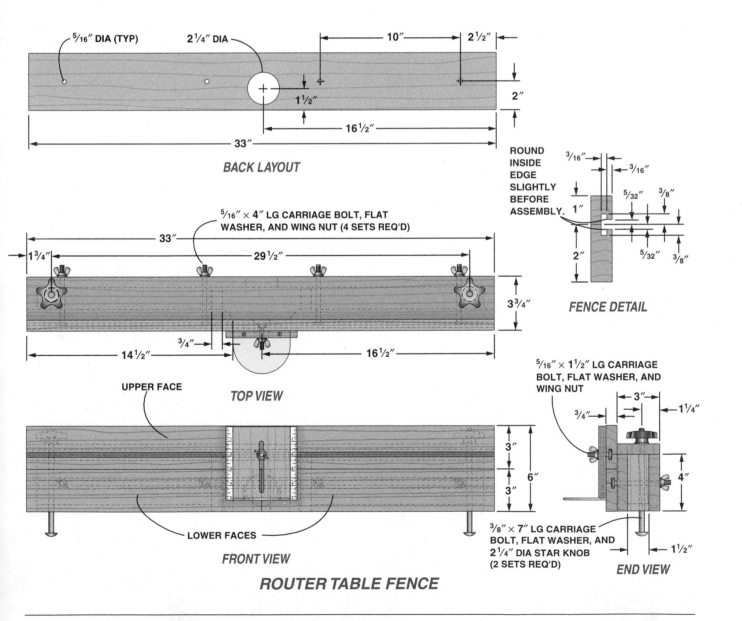

ROUTER TABLE FENCE

FENCE STOPS

Fence stops fasten to the fence on either side of the router bit, halting the cut at a particular spot. Make two, mirror images of each other, one to use to the right of the bit and the other to the left. Each stop is a single wood block held in place by a carriage bolt and wing nut. The head of the bolt slips into a T-slot in the upper fence; a dowel pin, also in the slot, keeps the stop vertical. Drill a hole through each stop from edge to edge, and countersink the hole on one edge. Tap #10-32 threads in the block, then drive a #10-32 flathead machine screw in the hole. This serves as a micro-adjustment. Because there are 32 threads per inch on the screw, one turn will move the head precisely ¹/₃₂ inch.

Remove the screw and cut two bevels in the edge that you countersunk to create a point. As you work, the sawdust piles up *behind* this point, keeping the dust from interfering with the accuracy of your work. When you thread the micro-adjustment screw back in its hole, the head should rest behind the point when bottomed out in the countersink.

STARTER PIN AND GUARD

To rout curved and contoured surfaces, you must use a *piloted* router bit. The pilot bearing, or on some older bits the pilot bushing, follows the edge. When you're using a table-mounted router, a starter pin helps begin the cut and guide the work. It also reduces the risk of kickback. The starter pin setup that Jim invented also includes a guard to reduce the danger of an uncovered router bit.

The starter pin is an automotive stud that threads into the mounting plate. A pair of jam nuts near the top of the pin supports a plastic guard. A second stud helps to stabilize the guard and keep it from turning. Stop nuts epoxied to the top ends of the studs make it easy to mount and dismount the assembly.

To mount this fixture, you must drill two holes in the mounting plate, then cut threads in the holes with a tap. A little paste wax on the tap helps you to cut smooth, crisp threads.

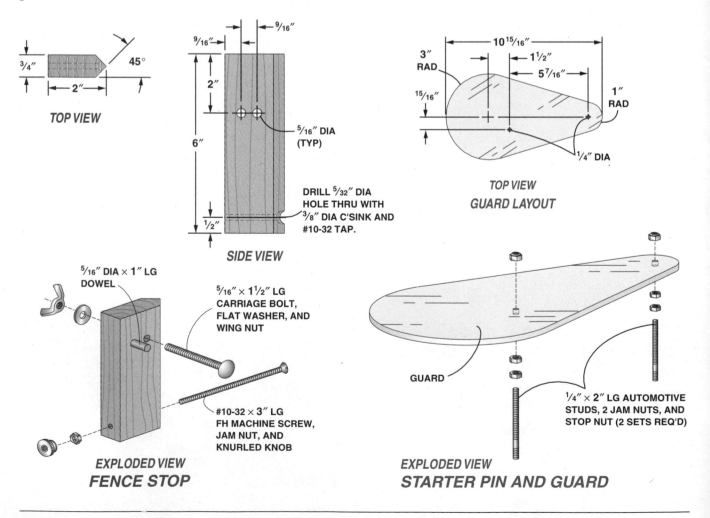

GUARD AND DEPTH GAUGE

After you "bury" the unused portion of a router bit in the fence, it's a good idea to cover the rest of it with a guard, if possible. This L-shaped guard fastens to the fence in the same T-slot that holds the stops.

If you want your guard to do double-duty as a gauge to measure the depth of cut, attach two scales, one at each edge. On one scale, turn the side with $\frac{1}{32}$-inch increments to the outside. On the other, turn the $\frac{1}{64}$ increments out. For most operations, $\frac{1}{32}$-inch accuracy is all you need, but the $\frac{1}{64}$-inch scale comes in handy from time to time.

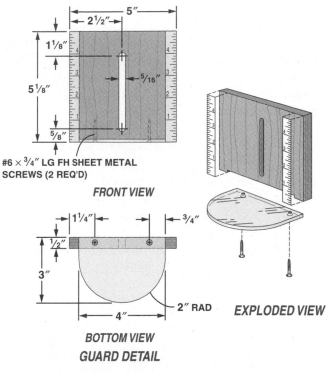

#6 × ¾" LG FH SHEET METAL SCREWS (2 REQ'D)

FRONT VIEW

BOTTOM VIEW
GUARD DETAIL

EXPLODED VIEW

GUARD AND DEPTH GAUGE

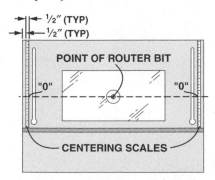

SCALE

GUARD

FENCE-POSITIONING SCALES

You can also use scales to help position the fence accurately, with a minimum of guesswork. You'll need two "centering" scales for this feature — rules on which the inch marks go right and left from zero. Rout shallow grooves for these scales near the right and left edges of the work surface.

Mount a pointed router bit in the router (such as a V-groove cutter), and adjust the depth of cut so the point is just below the surface. On the work surface, draw a straight line from right to left, perpendicular to the right and left edges. This line must pass through the point of the bit. Attach the scales to the work surface, aligning the "0" marks with the line you just drew.

½" (TYP)

½" (TYP)

POINT OF ROUTER BIT

"0"   "0"

CENTERING SCALES

RESOURCES

You can purchase self-stick centering scales from:

Woodworker's Supply, Inc.
1108 North Glenn Road
Casper, WY 82601

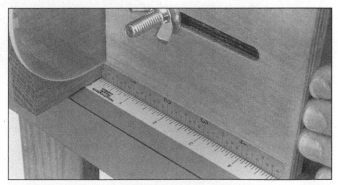

The increments on the fence-positioning centering scales are only $\frac{1}{16}$ inch. When you need more precision, use the Depth Gauge as a "vernier" scale. For example, to move the fence $\frac{1}{64}$ inch, place the depth gauge against the fence with a $\frac{1}{64}$-inch rule resting on the centering scale. Take note where one centering scale mark aligns with a gauge mark. Then move the fence so the same centering scale mark aligns with the next gauge mark. Do this for both ends of the fence.

TILT-TOP STAND

Jim calls it "praying to the router god." This is what most woodworkers have to do when they need to change a bit or make a depth-of-cut adjustment on their router table. They get down on their knees so they can reach under the table.

Well, there's no need for that anymore. Here's a practical, ergonomic design for a router table stand that allows you to change and adjust bits standing up, like the Deity intended. The top frame (which holds the work surface and the router) pivots at its back corners. The top assembly lifts up, and a support arm holds it in place at a comfortable angle. The collet, power switch, depth-of-cut lock, and all the controls rise up to meet you, visible and accessible.

Of course, to get this marvelous convenience, you have to build a complex mechanism, right? Nope. With just a few exceptions, the stand is made from rectangular parts. There is no joinery to speak of: All the parts are butt-jointed and joined with fasteners.

Two parts have rounded ends. The top ends of the back side legs are rounded to allow the top to pivot. The support arm is also rounded.

The support arm also displays the most complex bit of joinery — a J-slot (a long slot with a little hiccup at one end) as shown in the *Support Arm Layout* on page 119. Jim made the "hiccup" first by drilling a few overlapping holes to create a short slot. He routed the long slot perpendicular to it, then he cleaned up the edges of the short slot with a file.

To assemble the stand, glue the side legs to the front or back legs, creating L-shaped beams. Glue the cleats to the inside faces of the top frame members, then glue and screw the top frame together. Join the legs and stretchers with screws. If you wish, cut pieces of plywood and lay them on top of the stretchers to create storage shelves. Attach the top frame to the stand with bolts, flat washers, and stop nuts.

SHOP SAVVY

Whenever you use a metal bolt for a pivot, secure it with a stop nut. These special nuts have plastic rings around the inside to prevent the nuts from working loose. They are available in most hardware stores and automotive stores.

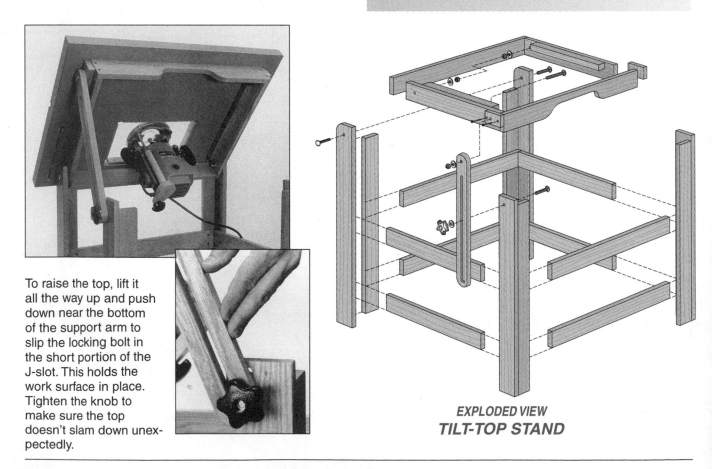

To raise the top, lift it all the way up and push down near the bottom of the support arm to slip the locking bolt in the short portion of the J-slot. This holds the work surface in place. Tighten the knob to make sure the top doesn't slam down unexpectedly.

EXPLODED VIEW
TILT-TOP STAND

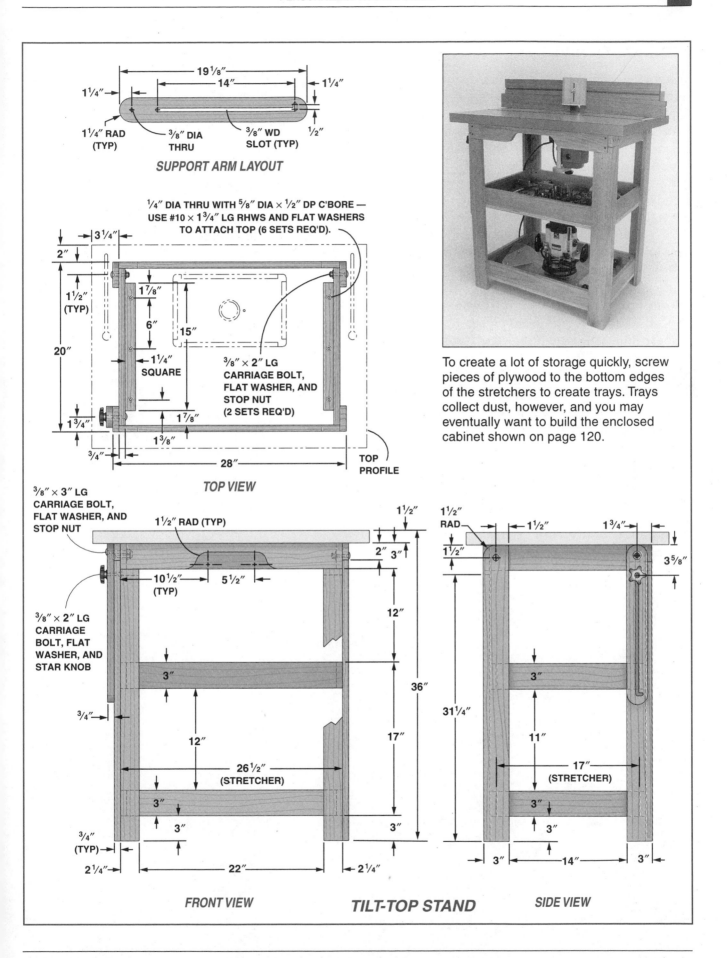

SUPPORT ARM LAYOUT

19⅛″
14″
1¼″
1¼″
1¼″ RAD (TYP)
⅜″ DIA THRU
⅜″ WD SLOT (TYP)
½″

¼″ DIA THRU WITH ⅝″ DIA × ½″ DP C'BORE — USE #10 × 1¾″ LG RHWS AND FLAT WASHERS TO ATTACH TOP (6 SETS REQ'D).

3¼″
2″
1½″ (TYP)
1⅞″
6″
15″
20″
1¼″ SQUARE
⅜″ × 2″ LG CARRIAGE BOLT, FLAT WASHER, AND STOP NUT (2 SETS REQ'D)
1¾″
1⅞″
1⅜″
¾″
28″
TOP PROFILE

TOP VIEW

To create a lot of storage quickly, screw pieces of plywood to the bottom edges of the stretchers to create trays. Trays collect dust, however, and you may eventually want to build the enclosed cabinet shown on page 120.

⅜″ × 3″ LG CARRIAGE BOLT, FLAT WASHER, AND STOP NUT
1½″ RAD (TYP)
1½″
2″ 3″
⅜″ × 2″ LG CARRIAGE BOLT, FLAT WASHER, AND STAR KNOB
10½″ (TYP)
5½″
12″
36″
¾″
12″
17″
26½″ (STRETCHER)
3″
3″
3″
¾″ (TYP)
2¼″
22″
2¼″

1½″ RAD
1½″
1¾″
1½″
3⅝″
31¼″
3″
11″
17″ (STRETCHER)
3″
3″ 3″
3″
14″
3″

FRONT VIEW   **TILT-TOP STAND**   **SIDE VIEW**

STORAGE CABINET

Although a couple of trays beneath the storage stand will provide a lot of storage space, a cabinet offers practical advantages beyond the fact that it looks nicer. First of all, it keeps the dust off the bits and accessories — an important consideration in any shop. Second, it strengthens the stand, making it more stable. Finally, it adds mass, especially when it's filled with accessories. This, too, increases the stability. The extra weight also decreases the noise and the annoying vibrations that you may hear and feel when routing.

This particular storage cabinet is barely worthy of the name "cabinet." It's more like a box, and a simple, open-ended box at that. Make the top, bottom, sides, and back from plywood; cut a few rabbet joints as shown in the *Back Corner Joinery Detail;* and assemble the parts with glue. Fasten the box to the inside surface of the legs by driving screws through the box sides and into the legs. The top of the box should be even with the top edges of the top stretchers of the Tilt-Top Stand on page 118.

Make the doors from sheets of plywood, and hang them on the front legs with flush-mount hinges. These hinges have thin leaves that fold into one another; therefore, they don't need to be mortised into the wood.

Perhaps the most complex element in the cabinet is the pullout shelf assembly. Cut grooves in the edges of the sliding sections and guide strips. Glue splines in the guide strips, and glue the strips to the fixed shelf. Slip the pullout shelves over the splines.

SAFEGUARD

The pullout shelf not only adds convenience, it adds safety. Why? Because you'll probably keep your router bits near the front of the shelf, where they are the most easily accessible. But when you need an accessory stored behind the bits, you'll have to reach over the sharp cutters into the murky no-man's land beyond. In doing so, your hand may catch on a sharp cutting flute and...OUCH! Like I said, the pullout shelf is a safety device.

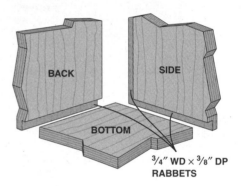

3/4" WD × 3/8" DP
RABBETS

*BACK CORNER
JOINERY DETAIL*

ANOTHER WAY TO GO

If you want, mount the sliding sections to the fixed shelf with full-extension slides. The advantage of this hardware is that it allows you to pull the half-shelves all the way out of the cabinet without detaching them. The disadvantage is that the slides are expensive.

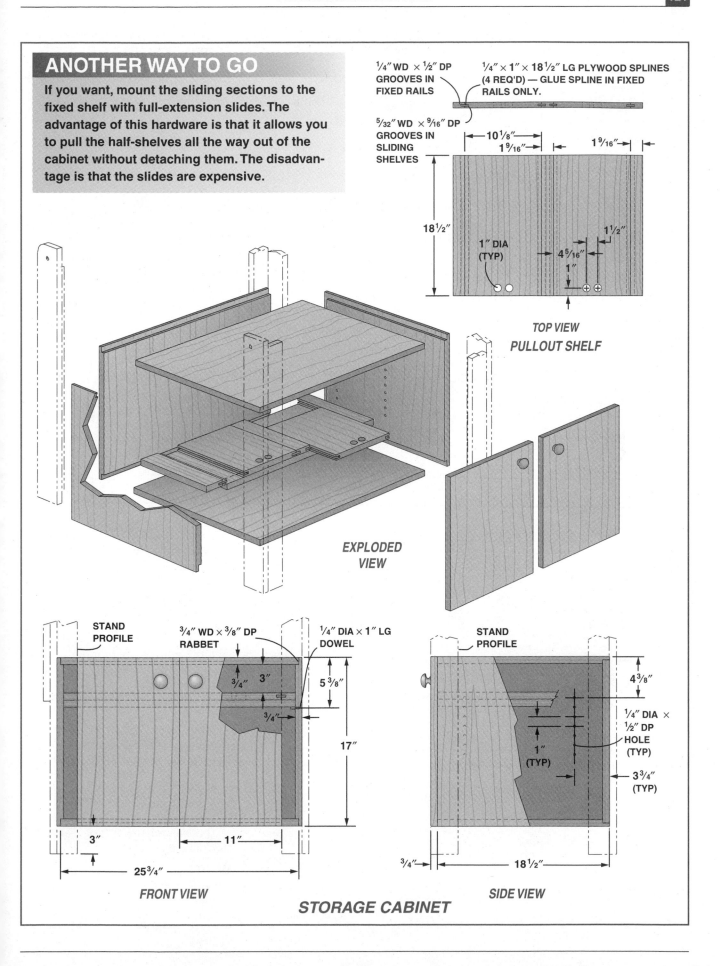

¼" WD × ½" DP GROOVES IN FIXED RAILS

¼" × 1" × 18½" LG PLYWOOD SPLINES (4 REQ'D) — GLUE SPLINE IN FIXED RAILS ONLY.

5/32" WD × 9/16" DP GROOVES IN SLIDING SHELVES

10⅛"
1 9/16"
1 9/16"
18½"
1" DIA (TYP)
4 5/16"
1½"
1"

TOP VIEW
PULLOUT SHELF

EXPLODED VIEW

STAND PROFILE
¾" WD × ⅜" DP RABBET
¼" DIA × 1" LG DOWEL
¾"
3"
¾"
5⅜"
17"
3"
11"
25¾"

FRONT VIEW

STAND PROFILE
4⅜"
¼" DIA × ½" DP HOLE (TYP)
1" (TYP)
3¾" (TYP)
¾"
18½"

SIDE VIEW

STORAGE CABINET

Index

A
Appliqués, 106

C
Chest
    box, assembly, 24
    box joinery, making, 12–23
    breadboard lid, making, 25
    drawer, making, 27, 28
    frame base, making, 24
    lid, hinging, 26
    materials, preparing, 9, 10
    size, 3, 4
    style, 5–7
Clock, grandfather
    assembly, 57, 58
    base, 57, 61–66
    bottom, false, 57, 66
    bracket feet, 57, 62, 63
    clock board, 58, 59
    clockwork, 52, 56, 58, 59
    columns, 57, 64, 71
    doors, 58, 64, 65, 69, 73
    finials, 71
    hood, 57, 58, 70–73
    materials, 59
    size, 51
    style, 53
    waist, 57, 66, 69, 70

D
Drawer, making, 27, 28, 44, 45

F
Finishing, 45, 73, 86, 106
Fireplace
    bump-out, making, 90, 107
    firebox, 89, 90, 93, 95, 107
    firewall, 89, 93, 95, 104, 105
    hearth, 103, 105, 106
    mantel, 88–107

G
Gluing, 35, 36, 61, 69, 95

J
Jigs and fixtures
    alignment gauge, 80
    dado-and-rabbet jig, 15, 17–20
    dovetail dust collector, 22
    dovetail jig, 44
    dovetail template, 19–22
    featherboard, 68
    fixed calipers, 42
    fluting jig, 97–99
    hinge-mounting jig, 26
    mortising template, 39
    parallel rule, 104
    pin-routing attachment, 85
    planing jig, 10, 48
    pusher, long, 68
    router crank, 113
    router jack, 113
    router table, jigs and fixtures, 108–121
    T-square guide, 13, 15, 26
    tenoning jig, 40
    trammel jig, 46–49
    scratch bead, 27, 28
Joinery
    box, 12–23, 95
    corner joints, 12, 13
    dado, 14–17
    dovetails, 12, 13, 18, 22, 23, 44, 45
    finger, 12
    floating joints, 12
    frame-and-panel, 64, 65, 96
    glue joint, 36
    groove, 12, 14–16
    lock joint, 12, 27, 28
    miter, 12, 69, 106
    mortise-and-tenon, 37–41
    pinned joint, 25
    rabbet, 12, 14–17
    tongue-and-dado, 80
    tongue-and-groove, 12

M
Mantel
    boxes, installing, 103
    boxes, making, 95
    columns, installing, 105
    columns, turning, 97
    finishing, 106, 107
    fireplace components, 89, 90, 93, 95, 103, 105–107
    installing, 105
    materials, preparing, 93, 95
    size, 89, 90
    style, 91
Materials, resources, 8, 22, 56, 106, 117

R
Router bits, types and uses, 14, 15, 22, 38, 48, 72, 83, 93, 96
Router table
    depth-of-cut adjusters, 113
    dust hookup, 114
    fences, 114, 115
    fence stops, 109, 116
    guard and depth gauge, 117
    mounting plate, 111, 112
    scales, 109, 117
    starter pin and guard, 109, 116
    storage cabinet, 109, 119–121
    tilt-top stand, 109, 118, 119
    torsion-box work surface, 109, 110
Routing
    dovetails, 18, 22, 44, 45
    flutes, 97, 98, 100
    gooseneck molding, 71, 72
    hardwoods and sheet materials, 93
    hinge mortises, 26
    molding, 67, 71, 72, 102
    mortises and tenons, 38–41
    pattern routing, 18, 75, 81–83
    pin routing, 84, 85
    rabbets, dadoes, and grooves, 14–17
    raised panels, 96
    secrets, 29
    spline grooves, 69
    stopped cuts, 16
    table tops, 43, 46–48
    thumbnail edge, 43
    turnings and cylinders, 100, 101

S
Shelves
    adjustable, 75
    assembling, 86
    decorative patterns, 81–86
    dimensions, standard, 75, 76
    joinery, cutting, 80, 81
    materials, preparing, 79, 80
    openwork, 75–77, 79, 81
    style, 77
    valance, bracing and moldings, making, 82
Skills
    correcting a loose tenon, 41
    cutting cove molding, 103, 104
    fixing sloppy dovetails, 23
    gluing up stock, 35, 36, 61, 95
    jointing with a router, 35
    making a cock bead, 27
    planing figured wood, 9, 10
    repairing a miter joint, 106
    sanding, saber saw, 87
    wrapping a board around a box, 9

T
Table
    apron, 36, 37, 41
    drawer making and fitting, 44, 45
    ergonomics, 32
    legs, duplicating, 41, 42
    legs, joinery, 37, 41
    legs, truing stock, 35
    materials, preparing, 35, 36
    top, gluing up, 35
    top, piecrust, scooping, 48
    top, porringer profile, cutting, 43
    top, round and oval, routing, 46–48
    top, thumbnail edge, routing 43
    size, 31, 32
    style, 33
Turning
    duplicating turned legs, 41, 42
    columns, 64, 71, 97, 98
    finials, 71
    gluing up stock, 95
    spindles, 97
    split columns, 64, 97, 98
    truing leg stock, 35

W
Wood
    busting up, 9
    figured, 9, 10
    shop-drying, 9

A few essential woodworking secrets...

Dress for success.

- Always wear eye protection — safety glasses for most operations, a full face shield for turning, routing, and other operations that throw wood chips. Always presume that every board you cut has a splinter with your name on it.

- Wear a dust mask when sanding and sawing — sawdust (especially fine sawdust) may be harmful to your lungs.

- Wear hearing protectors when routing or planing and for long, continuous power-tool operations. The high frequencies can harm your ears.

- Wear rubber gloves when handling dangerous chemicals — many of these can harm your skin or can be absorbed through the skin.

- Wear a vapor mask when finishing — the vapors of some finishing chemicals are potentially toxic.

- Wear close-fitting clothes with the sleeves rolled up above the elbows. Remove jewelry or anything that might catch on a tool.

Work smart.

- Install good lighting — it helps to see what you're doing.

- Hang or store tools within easy reach — the work goes faster.

- Keep your work area free of clutter — you don't want to trip when surrounded by sharp tools.

- Install a circuit breaker box within easy reach, and make sure each circuit is grounded and rated for sufficient amperage.

- Keep blades and cutters sharp and free of pitch — a dull tool is harder to control and therefore more dangerous than a sharp one.

- Keep arbors, tables, and fences properly aligned — misaligned tools are an accident waiting to happen.

- Keep tables and fences waxed and rust-free — this gives you more control over your work.

- Store flammable chemicals in fireproof containers. The same goes for shop rags. Some finishes generate heat as they cure and may cause rags to combust spontaneously.

Work safe.

- Keep the blade and cutter guards in place. They're like seat belts — they're a bother at first, but pretty soon you will feel uncomfortable without them.

- Mark the danger zones around blades and cutters, and keep your hands and fingers out of these areas.